D1522714

INTIMACY

A guided path to better intimacy in your marriage, both in and out of the bedroom

For Jewish Couples Seeking Connection

Workbook & Journal

the secrets of jewish women

Intimacy- A Guided Path to Better Intimacy In Your Marriage both In and Out of the Bedroom

(c)2022, Loujen Appraisal Processing and Administrative Services Inc DBA The Secrets Of Jewish Women, and its affiliates and assigns and licensors
All rights reserved
No text or images may be reproduced, transmitted or copied without the written consent of Loujen Appraisal Processing and Administrative Services Inc DBA The Secrets Of Jewish Women. Contravention is an infringement of the Copyright Act and its amendments and may be subject to legal action.

The Secrets Of Jewish Women is a Trademark of Loujen Appraisal Processing and Administrative Services Inc.
Trademarks may be registered in some jurisdictions.
All other trademarks are the property of their respective owners.

No claim to copyright is made for original U.S. Government Works.

RABBI YAAKOV HILLEL
ROSH YESHIVAT
HEVRAT AHAVAT SHALOM
45 ARZEY HABIRA ST. JERUSALEM

יעקב משה הלל
ראש ישיבת
חברת אהבת שלום
רח' ארזי הבירה 45 ירושלים

3 Tishre, 5784

A Letter of Blessing

To whom it may concern:

I have been personally acquainted with the Fraser family, both the parents and children, for many years. They are devoted to Torah and mitzvot and are outstanding supporters of institutions for the study and dissemination of Torah in America and Israel. In addition, they dedicate time to *zikuy harabbim*, benefitting and bringing merit to the community. As Hazal teach, those who give of themselves for the benefit of the community will be granted much blessing and be protected from harm.

Mrs. Fraser, a certified *kallah* teacher who coaches Jewish couples, is currently writing a guide for Jewish couples seeking connection, or in other words, *shalom bayit*. Drawing upon her experience of situations in her own life and family and the numerous families she has counseled, she presents a commonsense approach to a wide variety of topics, including relationships within the family, finances, and much more.

Mrs. Fraser's book is not a halachic work and as such, does not really require a rabbinic approbation. A work of halachah deals with straightforward halachic rulings and how they are applied in specific cases, often taking into consideration the community or individual for whom the ruling is given. Mrs. Fraser's book instead speaks to readers as a friend, offering her own experience and guidance to couples seeking advice in the crucial area of *shalom bayit* and building a good, happy Jewish marriage and family.

May Hashem bless the author, her husband, and the entire family with a good, heathy, and happy new year. May all her efforts on behalf of the community be a source of blessing and benefit to all.

Rabbi Yaakov Hillel

R' Yaakov Hillel

Rabbi Zev Leff	הרב זאב לף
Rabbi of Moshav Matityahu	מרא דאתרא מושב מתתיהו
Rosh HaYeshiva—Yeshiva Gedola Matityahu	ראש הישיבה—ישיבה גדולה מתתיהו

D.N. Modiin	פקס': 08-976-5326 :ıx	ד.נ. מודיעין 71917

Dear Friends,

I have read the book "Intimacy for Jewish Couples Seeking Connection" by Mrs. Sarah Fraser. The material is presented to choson and kallah teachers to enrich their ability to prepare grooms and brides for marriage and to enable them to continue to guide and acclimate the new couple through the first three months of their married life.

I found the material to be based on solid Torah ideas and ideals. It is presented in a manner that speaks to this generation in their language and prepares them with the instruction needed for establishing a healthy foundation for their marriage. This enables couples to learn the foundations of a healthy marriage and proper intimacy from reliable sources and not have to seek direction "on line" from dubious and distorted sources.

The book is divided between informative chapters followed by workbook sessions in which the participants are asked to record personal answers to questions pertinent to that chapter that can give them awareness to their own feelings and reveal various areas of concern that can be addressed with professional help. The sessions are meant to both give guidance to avoid problems and challenges that new couples can experience, but also to discover the roots of those problems and challenges in the perspective grooms and brides and enable the choson and kallah teachers to refer the couple to Rabbonim, therapists, and medical professionals to help facilitate healthy solutions to those problems.

Marriage is a holy and very important foundation of society in general and especially in Judaism. As such, it needs spiritual, emotional, and physical preparation and guidance. This is especially necessary now at a time where the very institution of marriage is being threatened in portions of secular society and whose very foundation is being attacked with serious sexual, gender and core values aberrations. Mrs. Fraser, a certified kallah teacher and intimacy coach for Jewish couples is herself a successful wife and mother whom with I am personally acquainted.

I feel that when used properly together with Rabbinic and professional guidance this program will contribute to strengthening marriage and stemming the high divorce rate unfortunately prevalent even in the observant Jewish community.

I commend the authoress for a well planned, quality presentation and program and pray to Hashem that her efforts are met with success and that she and her family are blessed with life and health and the wherewithal to continue to merit the community.

Sincerely,
With Torah blessings

Rabbi Zev Leff

LEARNING PATH

OUR VISION

Our vision is to enable couples to focus on their marriage and on each other. We do this by creating important conversations that otherwise may be avoided. Our objective is to remove all of the noise, chaos and confusion of daily life by turning the couple back to the original purpose for which they were inspired to spend their lives together.

Please note, this workbook is best utilized in conjunction with a separate notebook or journal.

OUR MISSION

Our mission is to provide a unique and sorely needed resource for all those individuals dealing in and/ or with strengthening Jewish marriages in these difficult times.

FOR COUNSELORS

Your clients will be best served by reading and answering the questions in each of the chapters and sending back their answers prior to sessions. This will facilitate clarity where the couple is not aligned. You will see the benefit of using this framework as it will cut down on useless sidetracking which leads into irrelevant topics and unproductive venting.

FOR CHOSSON AND KALLAH TEACHERS

This course and workbook are professional teaching tools. Newlyweds repeatedly seek help and counseling during the first years of their marriage. They need guidance on how to live cooperatively and on intimacy issues. Unfortunately couples stop talking to each other and suffer in silence for fear of creating an argument. Not knowing how to initiate intimate conversations on their own, they often retreat and avoid one another. Facilitating communication between couples is a skill that needs to be worked. It's a service that creates the space for exceptional listening to occur in place of silence and avoidance. Reducing anxiety with this method will establish a stabilizing effect on the couple and their children, and create a harmonious atmosphere in the home for all.

FOR COUPLES

The questions presented will provide both focus and clarity when used as journaling prompts. The exercise of writing the answers is more beneficial than just thinking about them alone. This is especially important when done with one's partner. Couples undertaking the course alone are strongly encouraged to engage a competent coach who can guide them through any concerns that may arise. This course is a framework for interactive conversations between couples to get to know each other better and establish a deeper bond. We understand that many couples may not have had extensive experience dating. People often get married having had little communication with the opposite sex. Intimacy starts with listening and a genuine desire to understand one's partner. Understanding starts with asking open-ended questions which may be tough. This moves both people to greater honesty and introspection and helps give clear insights into how the other person thinks.

the secrets of jewish women

WHY

For Yourself

A happy marriage is at the center of a happy life. A gratifying marriage has been shown to improve mental health, reduce depression, anxiety and addictions.

For Your Family

A happy marriage can increase the cognitive and emotional well being of children. A home free of anxiety and tension promotes creativity and self-confidence.

For Life

Your relationship with your spouse affects all areas of your life. A supportive partner leads to more success in your career and can bring you closer to Gd. Honesty about who you are and a commitment to growing with your partner will lead to family values that pass down for generations to come. Your marriage is important and worth the investment.

DISCLAIMER

*This workbook is intended for both women and men. While there are some references geared more towards one gender, the information and suggestions provided are still relevant.

This workbook is not intended to be used as a Halachic guide or in lieu of Rabbinic guidance.

It should be mentioned that the Shulchan Aruch instructs couples as to the manner in which Intimacy should be carried out. Couples should inquire with their Rav as to how those instructions apply to their specific situation.

This book contains graphic material.

the secrets of jewish women

INTRODUCTION

The secret to long lasting love is making dedicated time for one another a priority and never ceasing to ask the right questions.

Establishing and maintaining a healthy marriage is hard. That's just a fact. A good marriage is not made by chance. It's a choice. Successful marriages are created every day through seemingly small acts of love, small gestures and words of affirmation. Learning about your partner is an ongoing action. Maintaining curiosity about who your partner is and sharing who you are is vital. No relationship is perfect. There will naturally be conflict. Conflict in its highest purpose illuminates and invites a deepening of connection, belonging, and safety. Love is a practice in how to express and receive loving attention.

Sarah Fraser

CHAPTER 1

COMMITMENT

Commitment is a choice we make in our marriage. Remaining physically faithful is not enough. Showing our partner their importance in our life is the central component of commitment. Trustworthiness in a marriage means that you are who you say you are and you do what you say you are going to do. It means taking accountability for your actions. When tired, overworked or just distracted, we need to stop what we are doing and acknowledge the person across from us. This could look like a simple conversation, a hug or a smile. Whatever the moment calls for, we authentically try to deliver and show up for our partner.

QUESTIONS ON COMMITMENT

1. Refer back to your family of origin; this was your first example of marriage. How did your family values influence your view of marriage? For the good and bad?
2. How do you see yourself in a marriage? Will you assume traditional gender roles? How will that affect your identity?
3. Is there something missing in your "sense of self" that you hope your partner will fulfill?
4. What persona / self-image did you create to navigate single life? What kind of partner did you think you would attract?
5. Did you have many relationships before marriage? How did you come to decide this was your person?
6. If yes, what patterns of behavior were necessary during those relationships? What patterns did you maintain? What did you leave behind? Why?
7. Are there things about your single life that you miss? What are they? How can you incorporate them into your marriage together?
8. Now that you're married, what do you really want from this relationship? Are you aware of what your partner wants? What is that?
9. How do you see your life together now that you're not alone?

1. Refer back to your family of origin; this was your first example of marriage. How did your family values influence your view of marriage? For the good and bad?

_____

_____

_____

_____

_____

_____

_____

_____

_____

_____

_____

_____

_____

_____

_____

_____

2. How do you see yourself in a marriage? Will you assume traditional gender roles? How will that affect your identity?

_____

_____

_____

_____

_____

_____

_____

_____

_____

_____

_____

_____

_____

_____

3. Is there something missing in your "sense of self" that you hope your partner will fulfill?

_____

_____

_____

_____

_____

_____

_____

_____

_____

_____

_____

_____

_____

_____

4. What persona / self-image did you create to navigate single life? What kind of partner did you think you would attract?

_____

_____

_____

_____

_____

_____

_____

_____

_____

_____

_____

_____

_____

5. Did you have many relationships before marriage? How did you come to decide this was your person?

_____

_____

_____

_____

_____

_____

_____

_____

_____

_____

_____

_____

_____

_____

6. If yes, what patterns of behavior were necessary during those relationships? What patterns did you maintain? What did you leave behind? Why?

_____

_____

_____

_____

_____

_____

_____

_____

_____

_____

_____

_____

_____

7. Are there things about your single life that you miss? What are they? How can you incorporate them into your marriage together?

_____

_____

_____

_____

_____

_____

_____

_____

_____

_____

_____

_____

_____

_____

8. Now that you're married, what do you really want from this relationship? Are you aware of what your partner wants? What is that?

_____

_____

_____

_____

_____

_____

_____

_____

_____

_____

_____

_____

_____

_____

9. How do you see your life together now that you're not alone?

_____

_____

_____

_____

_____

_____

_____

_____

_____

_____

_____

_____

_____

_____

COMMITMENT

Marriage is a lifelong commitment that requires mutual love, support, and dedication from both partners.

Sometimes, we think of commitment as just being physically committed, but it is more than that. We need to be emotionally committed as well. That means avoiding deep meaningful or personal conversations with members of the opposite sex. Unfortunately, many couples struggle with commitment issues in marriage that make it difficult to maintain a healthy and fulfilling relationship. Commitment issues can be caused by fear of the unknown, fear of abandonment, fear of failure and even fear of the future. As a result the couple may have difficulty expressing their love and understanding for one another, making it difficult to form a strong bond.

In order to address commitment issues in marriage, couples must first be willing to communicate openly. It requires being vulnerable and sharing personal thoughts and feelings that you would not share with a stranger or someone you don't deem trustworthy. It is essential that both parties are able to express their feelings fully and find a way to better understand each other, to work together and build a strong, lasting connection. It's critical to navigate and manage expectations, talk through fears and work towards solutions together.

Couples must realize that it's okay to make mistakes and that mistakes are part of the learning process in any relationship. No one is perfect, not even you, we all make mistakes.

Remaining open to forgiveness, learning how to apologize, and how to move past mistakes is a necessary part of any marriage.

Be sure to make time for one another and express your love and appreciation for each other on a regular basis. This can be achieved through quality time spent doing things that you both enjoy and expressing your feelings for one another verbally.

Even if a couple is struggling with commitment issues in marriage, it is important to realize that marriage is a constant work in progress. It takes time to get to know each other and acclimated to the different ways each person does things.

Curiosity and asking open ended questions goes a long way in establishing communication. Open ended questions require more than a simple yes or no answer. The goal is to develop a better understanding of how your partner thinks.

Sarah Fraser

CHAPTER 2

CONFLICT

No two people are going to agree on everything. The goal of any conflict is to understand this unique, complex and amazing person to whom you are married. One myth about marriage is that *if you never fight, that means you have a good relationship.* It's just not true and the best time to address how you're going to deal with conflict is not in the middle of an argument. Conflict is natural, and when addressed with love and understanding can deepen trust. Mutual understanding is the end goal of any conflict. Some problems will never be solved - you are two different people, with two different pasts. The ability to manage these differences with respect is key to living peacefully.

"Trouble brings experience, and experience brings wisdom."
-Yiddish proverb

QUESTIONS ON CONFLICT

1. How have our upbringing in families of origin created default patterns of either being avoidant or anxious in dealing with our conflicts?
2. How can we accept each other? If we believe that Gd put us together with a higher purpose, how can we use that knowledge to truly accept each other's differences without trying to change one another?
3. How did it affect you when there was conflict in your family? How did you react?
4. How do you express anger? Are you aware of when you are becoming angry?
5. What are your specific triggers? Do you know how to stop your anger from becoming rage?
6. How do we settle a disagreement? How long does it take before we are willing to compromise and move on?
7. What are some of your biggest fears in life?
8. Is there something bothering you that you would like to have addressed?
9. What will happen if we don't change? What will it cost us?
10. What are we willing to sacrifice to change?
11. What is a boundary that is non-negotiable for you?
12. What do we now understand about each other and ourselves that we did not before?
13. What strategies can we come up with to protect our children from our conflicts?

1. How have our upbringing in families of origin created default patterns of either being avoidant or anxious in dealing with our conflicts?

_____

_____

_____

_____

_____

_____

_____

_____

_____

_____

_____

_____

_____

_____

2. How can we accept each other? If we believe that Gd put us together with a higher purpose, how can we use that knowledge to truly accept each other's differences without trying to change one another?

_____

_____

_____

_____

_____

_____

_____

_____

_____

_____

_____

_____

3. How did it affect you when there was conflict in your family? How did you react?

_____

_____

_____

_____

_____

_____

_____

_____

_____

_____

_____

_____

_____

4. How do you express anger? Are you aware of when you are becoming angry?

_____

_____

_____

_____

_____

_____

_____

_____

_____

_____

_____

_____

_____

5. What are your specific triggers? Do you know how to stop your anger from becoming rage?

_____

_____

_____

_____

_____

_____

_____

_____

_____

_____

_____

_____

_____

_____

6. How do we settle a disagreement? How long does it take before we are willing to compromise and move on?

_____

_____

_____

_____

_____

_____

_____

_____

_____

_____

_____

_____

_____

7. What are some of your biggest fears in life?

_____

_____

_____

_____

_____

_____

_____

_____

_____

_____

_____

_____

_____

8. Is there something bothering you that you would like to have addressed?

_____

_____

_____

_____

_____

_____

_____

_____

_____

_____

_____

_____

_____

9. What will happen if we don't change? What will it cost us?

_____

_____

_____

_____

_____

_____

_____

_____

_____

_____

_____

_____

_____

10. What are we willing to sacrifice to change?

_____

_____

_____

_____

_____

_____

_____

_____

_____

_____

_____

_____

_____

11. What is a boundary that is non-negotiable for you?

_____

_____

_____

_____

_____

_____

_____

_____

_____

_____

_____

_____

_____

_____

12. What do we now understand about each other and ourselves that we did not before?

---

13. What strategies can we come up with to protect our children from our conflicts?

NOTES

CONFLICT

Before we can talk about resolving a conflict, we need to discuss what conflict is.

To make things simple we are going to talk about two people with a problem that surfaces. Another way to look at conflict is to understand it as a circumstance that appears suddenly that nobody is ready for or knows what to do with.

Let's just say the circumstance appears and makes itself known, catching both people off guard.

What happens next is classic. Person A has thoughts and feelings which cause a reaction and ultimately a behavior. This behavior is usually not acceptable to Person B. This goes both ways pretty much simultaneously. The circumstance is what lies between them.

The expectations of both people shift the blame back and forth from; "You fix it, I don't like this and I don't know what to do with this." To "you did this and it's all your fault."

At this point the circumstance just sits there with no solution in sight. What is happening is that the circumstance has just grown in proportion with the anxiety and tension of both people involved.

They both buffer around the circumstance with varying instilled behaviors that they learned from childhood.

Please note; the following is an oversimplification of a very complicated dynamic.

The classic two behaviors are anxious and avoidant. Both are coming from childhood wounds where the child had to protect themselves from ongoing situations in the home and at school where they felt powerless.

The first child's response to this uncontrollable situation was to become anxious. Fearful of abandonment, they retreated, mainly functioning under the radar so as not to be seen. They develop overdependence and cling to significant figures as if their lives depend on it. This person will naturally disengage from conflict completely and try to people-please and be silent.

The second child, the avoidant, is also fearful of abandonment and in response creates a wall. This defense mechanism of protection helps them isolate from the environment that they cannot control. This person will naturally stay and contend from a distance behind their self-made wall. Most interactions come from a place of fight or flight response and under duress.

These two personality types generally marry one another through a trauma based connection.

In conflict resolution what is required when this unfortunate circumstance surfaces is that both people stay in their own lane. Self regulation means introspection, and thinking silently to oneself.

Allowing space, letting the other person know you need time to think alone and telling them that you will be right back shows them respect. Whoever initiates the separation has the obligation to return within an hour or less, or there is a risk in alienating the other person unintentionally. Once you reconvene, you will have gained a more accurate perspective
and you will be capable of resolving the conflict.

The expectations each one has of the other is the actual problem. Expecting that another person will react to bad news our way, limits our ability to see from their perspective . The idea of how to solve the problem comes from the assumption that the problem is somehow not our own. The lack of emotional maturity escalates and increases the original circumstance and adds unnecessary fuel to the fire.

Staying quiet within oneself and introspection is an art worth cultivating. However, the silent treatment is abusive and punishes our partner, even if that is not your original intention. Our silence is actually speaking volumes about our inability to effectively communicate. Asking our partner for an uninterrupted minute or two to speak, not only creates space for them to hear your concerns but also for you to hear yourself for the first time on the matter. Once you "get it out", say no more. Make sure when you're speaking, it's ALL of it. Now, it's their turn to respond and no matter what they say, you don't defend, judge them or justify yourself. You listen quietly and intently to their point of view with the intention of truly trying to understand. At this point, neither of you agree with each other- that's ok! You just succeeded in true communication.

Love and good intentions go right out the window the minute the unexpected shows up. Using the prefrontal cortex*, which is the decision making part of the brain, is an exercise worth practicing.

*In order to access the prefrontal cortex, awareness of the behavior comes first. The decision to change and the necessary steps one has to employ for the new behavior to take effect starts with recognizing the negative outcome of our behavior.

*COGNITIVE BEHAVIOR PRACTICE

- I see my behavior is hurting this person, I commit to not yelling or raising my voice.
- I will be mindful of where I feel triggered in my body, take note of that feeling and where it's located. I commit to changing my default reaction.

There are no marriages without chaos and pain. Recognizing and becoming aware that you're triggered, knowing yourself and your patterns of behavior, are crucial to ensuring emotional health and wellbeing. You cannot depend on another to do this work for you.

Conflict resolution guide:

- Understand and acknowledge the problem... The fact that there is a problem here. Before taking any action to resolve the conflict, seek to understand the situation in your own mind and your partner's opinion.
- Talk openly and honestly. Each person has a right to be heard and to express their thoughts and feelings. Speak respectfully and don't interrupt one another. Intently listen to your partner to gain a better understanding.
- Practice empathy. Feel what your partner is feeling. This leads to deeper understanding and better insight into the issue.
- Reach for a compromise when a total agreement seems too far off. With the understanding established above, both parties must show willingness to meet in the middle.
- Take short breaks. This will leave room to gain a fresh perspective on the situation and help you reach an agreement.
- Practice active problem solving. Discuss various options and plan out solutions together.
- If a resolution cannot be made; seek out professional help. Go to a coach or counselor who can offer a fresh and unbiased opinion. This will no doubt lead to a more effective solution.

Sarah Fraser

CHAPTER 3

SPIRITUAL, EMOTIONAL, MENTAL AND PHYSICAL WELLNESS

You are not your body. You are not your thoughts. You are but a witness to this beautiful, tragic, hilarious human experience. You are part and parcel to life itself. The very breath within you is of Gd. You are no accident and you have a purpose. The question is; can you identify and live within that purpose? The endless search for meaning is constant and without purpose can lead to compulsion. Compulsive behaviors, addictions, overeating, overworking, overdrinking, porn etc. can be overcome. When you start to believe in the ability to separate your thoughts from your actions, problems naturally become smaller and solutions come into view. Compulsive behaviors are chasing a real need that is being suppressed. Do not seek to kill the need itself. Rather examine the need. Nurture it in a healthy and constructive way that serves your true purpose.

QUESTIONS ON WELLNESS

1. What is addiction? Where does it come from?
2. How do people become addicted?
3. Have you had times when you ended up engaging in your negative behavior more, or longer, than you intended?
4. Have you more than once wanted to cut down or stop your negative behavior, or tried to, but couldn't?
5. Have you wanted to engage in your behavior so badly you couldn't think of anything else?
6. Have you found that engaging in your behavior often interferes with taking care of your home or family? Has this caused career troubles or financial problems?
7. Have you continued to engage in your behavior even though it was making you feel depressed, anxious or adding to another health problem?
8. Are you secretive about your behavior? Do you lie to cover it up?
9. Do you ever think about your purpose in life?
10. Are you living in and serving that purpose?
11. Are your beliefs about yourself aligned with your desired results?
12. How do you stay motivated to maintain a healthy lifestyle?
13. What steps do you take in managing any chronic health issues you may have?
14. What boundaries do you set to manage your emotional wellbeing?
15. What hobbies or activities do you engage in to boost your

mood?

1. What is addiction? Where does it come from?

2. How do people become addicted?

_____

_____

_____

_____

_____

_____

_____

_____

_____

_____

_____

_____

_____

3. Have you had times when you ended up engaging in your negative behavior more, or longer, than you intended?

_____

_____

_____

_____

_____

_____

_____

_____

_____

_____

_____

_____

_____

_____

4. Have you more than once wanted to cut down or stop your negative behavior, or tried to, but couldn't?

_____

_____

_____

_____

_____

_____

_____

_____

_____

_____

_____

_____

_____

5. Have you wanted to engage in your behavior so badly you couldn't think of anything else?

_____

_____

_____

_____

_____

_____

_____

_____

_____

_____

_____

_____

_____

6. Have you found that engaging in your behavior often interferes with taking care of your home or family? Has this caused career troubles or financial problems?

_____

_____

_____

_____

_____

_____

_____

_____

_____

_____

_____

_____

_____

7. Have you continued to engage in your behavior even though it was making you feel depressed, anxious or adding to another health problem?

_____

_____

_____

_____

_____

_____

_____

_____

_____

_____

_____

_____

_____

_____

8. Are you secretive about your behavior? Do you lie to cover it up?

_____

_____

_____

_____

_____

_____

_____

_____

_____

_____

_____

_____

_____

9. Do you ever think about your purpose in life?

_____

_____

_____

_____

_____

_____

_____

_____

_____

_____

_____

_____

_____

_____

10. Are you living in and serving that purpose?

_____

_____

_____

_____

_____

_____

_____

_____

_____

_____

_____

_____

_____

11. Are your beliefs about yourself aligned with your desired results?

12. How do you stay motivated to maintain a healthy lifestyle?

_____

_____

_____

_____

_____

_____

_____

_____

_____

_____

_____

_____

13. What steps do you take in managing any chronic health issues you may have?

_____

_____

_____

_____

_____

_____

_____

_____

_____

_____

_____

_____

_____

_____

14. What boundaries do you set to manage your emotional wellbeing?

_____

_____

_____

_____

_____

_____

_____

_____

_____

_____

_____

_____

_____

15. What hobbies or activities do you engage in to boost your mood?

_____

_____

_____

_____

_____

_____

_____

_____

_____

_____

_____

_____

_____

_____

NOTES

Spiritually

Strive to provide each other with spiritual nourishment and growth. This does not necessarily mean that the couple must share the same outlook. They must be willing to support each other's beliefs and respect each other's rights to pursue their own spiritual path. Additionally, it means that the couple create a safe and encouraging atmosphere where they can openly discuss their faith and any issues that may arise because of it. Just because your perspectives may differ doesn't mean you can't have a strong connection. Try to express your opinion in a way that doesn't attack or belittle the other person's belief system. Let your partner grow spiritually.

A couple can create a spiritual atmosphere in the house for children by setting an example of peacefulness, mindfulness and gratitude. Taking your time while lighting candles for Shabbat will create a spiritual environment the kids will feel. Explaining self reflection and having encouraging conversations about spirituality creates awareness of gratitude and can change the atmosphere in the household.

As a parent, it is important to lead your children spiritually. Even if you don't consider yourself "religious" it is important to provide ethical guidance and moral instruction as part of a child's education. Leading by example parents can provide children with a precedent of spiritual living that will set them on the right path.

One way to lead spiritually is to practice what you preach. Practice Torah Values and beliefs that you hope to instill in your children. Upholding the ideals of honesty, kindness and respect show your children that you are living according to your beliefs. Encouraging children's curiosity about spiritual matters is important guidance for the rest of their lives.

Emotionally

Maintaining emotional wellbeing in a relationship can feel overwhelming. While difficult to do, one must not take total responsibility for the other person's moods.

On the one hand, we must be sensitive to our partner's triggers and feelings while on the other, not bear responsibility for their temper which is ultimately their choice.

When we commit to marriage, we commit to the growth of ourselves and our partners. It is imperative to show sensitivity and to have responsible, open communication. Showing respect for each other's opinions, beliefs and feelings without control or manipulation is crucial. It is important to maintain your own identity outside of the relationship. Make sure you nurture your separate interests, careers and activities.

Spend quality time together. Take the time to really be with each other and not just in the same space. Talk, laugh, be silly and really engage with one another.

Men can achieve emotional wellness in a marriage by communicating openly and honestly with their partner. This needs to be learned as it is not a natural state for a man. Expressing emotions in a healthy way while listening and validating their partners feelings and needs creates emotional intimacy. Juggling the delicate balance between work, play, family and being a husband is quite an undertaking.

Women can show emotional wellness in marriage by expressing their feelings openly and not avoiding difficult conversations with silence. Rewarding themselves often with self care activities will go a long way in recognizing their own self-worth. Celebrating their partners accomplishments and making physical connection a priority will stabilize and enhance the emotional connection.

Mentally

Maintaining mental health is vital for a successful relationship. Mental health conditions such as depression, anxiety, bipolar etc. can put a strain on any relationship. If these conditions are not addressed, couples may have difficulty communicating and resolving conflict. Unresolved conflict leads to feelings of resentment, alienation, and unhappiness. Both partners must work together and separately to manage their own mental health. One must be mindful of each individual's mental health, particularly in challenging times like after childbirth, following the loss of a loved one or even during financial stress.

It is also important to practice self-care. Taking steps to maintain a healthy lifestyle like engaging in regular physical activity, having good nutrition and sufficient rest go a long way in maintaining a balanced mind.

Some tips for maintaining a healthy, balanced lifestyle.

Meal Prepping

At the beginning of each week, cook and prepare daily portions for lunches and dinners. This will help you save time, save money and best manage portion size.

3x Weekly Physical Activity

Regular physical activity has been proven to reduce stress, tension and mental fatigue. It can boost energy levels and will leave you feeling less angry and frustrated.

Getting Good Sleep

The mental benefits of sleep are thought to include the capacity to improve creativity for problem solving, lower the likelihood of depression and other mental disorders, and even increase life expectancy.

Physically

Make exercise a priority. Schedule time to work out together, or find ways to stay active like taking walks or joining a local gym or recreational sports activity.
Eat healthy meals and snacks. Try to make it a point to sit down and enjoy meals together. Making healthy choices when it comes to food has the biggest impact on your physical health.

Make wellness a priority. Incorporate healthy activities into the routine of your relationship such as yoga, meditation or massage.

Utilize social support. Spend time with friends, family, or other couples who can provide support and help you stay connected to each other.

The physical health of one partner can have a significant impact psychologically and physically on everyone. If one person is suffering from a chronic condition, it can lead to additional stress and worry for the other. It's especially important that the condition is managed properly. This added stress can lead to symptoms of depression, fatigue and irritability for both parties. To address the issues it is important that the sick partner takes steps to look after their physical health and prioritize themselves. This may include exercise, healthy eating, maintaining an active social life or working with a professional to better manage the condition.
It is also important for the well person to take care of themselves. This may include seeking professional help if needed, and being supportive of the partner suffering from the actual health issue.

*Intimacy encompasses all aspects of wellness; spiritual, emotional, mental and especially physical.

Take time to physically relax your own body in a bath, shower or have a massage.

This helps to calm down the nervous system and create awareness of your bodily sensations.

Use this time to fantasize about a future, pleasurable, physical experience you and your partner will have . Slow your mind down and use your memory to access a last encounter.

Just being in this pleasant space will release dopamine.

Dopamine plays an important role in executive function, motor control, motivation and arousal.

Sarah Fraser

CHAPTER 4

WEIGHT MANAGEMENT

We live in a 24 hour time frame. The body has 3 specific jobs in relation to food processing.
There is an intake cycle, assimilation cycle, and an elimination cycle.

Weight gain occurs when the body has to slow down during the assimilation or elimination cycle to absorb incoming food. Food eaten during these times is stored as fat while the body continues to do its job.
Unless this is understood, you will never permanently lose weight.
The best short-term solution for faster weight loss is putting the body into a state of Ketosis whereby it uses stored fat as fuel.
This method can be used for faster results after childbirth, for an upcoming special event, vacation or if you are generally in need of a change in your relationship with food.

QUESTIONS ON
WEIGHT

1. Are you eating out of hunger or habit? Do you know when you're full? Are you aware that there is a feeling associated with hunger and fullness? Did you know that it's the same feeling?
2. Are you seeking nurturing or nourishment when you choose what to eat?
3. Are you really hungry? Or perhaps angry, anxious, lonely or tired?
4. What do you want to feel when you eat? Satiated? Or is there something else?
5. Are you procrastinating? From what? Why?
6. Do you have feelings of guilt, shame, or embarrassment about your weight or the way you eat?
7. Do you eat the same way in front of others as you do when you are alone?
8. Is your eating affecting your health or the way you live your life? Do you find yourself eating too much and throwing up? Then repeating the cycle?
9. When your weight is up or down, does it affect your self confidence? How? Why?
10. Do you find yourself attractive when you look in the mirror? Are you comparing yourself to an unattainable image of perfection? Can you adjust your mindset to feel truly sexy as you are? (If the answer is no, we need to address this.)
11. Does your partner comment on your body positively or negatively? Do you make similar comments?

1. Are you eating out of hunger or habit? Do you know when you're full? Are you aware that there is a feeling associated with hunger and fullness? Did you know that it's the same feeling?

_____

_____

_____

_____

_____

_____

_____

_____

_____

_____

_____

_____

_____

_____

_____

2. Are you seeking nurturing or nourishment when you choose what to eat?

_____

_____

_____

_____

_____

_____

_____

_____

_____

_____

_____

_____

_____

3. Are you really hungry? Or perhaps angry, anxious, lonely or tired?

_____

_____

_____

_____

_____

_____

_____

_____

_____

_____

_____

_____

_____

_____

4. What do you want to feel when you eat? Satiated? Or is there something else?

_____

_____

_____

_____

_____

_____

_____

_____

_____

_____

_____

_____

5. Are you procrastinating? From what? Why?

6. Do you have feelings of guilt, shame, or embarrassment about your weight or the way you eat?

_____

_____

_____

_____

_____

_____

_____

_____

_____

_____

_____

_____

7. Do you eat the same way in front of others as you do when you are alone?

_____

_____

_____

_____

_____

_____

_____

_____

_____

_____

_____

_____

_____

8. Is your eating affecting your health or the way you live your life? Do you find yourself eating too much and throwing up? Then repeating the cycle?

_____

_____

_____

_____

_____

_____

_____

_____

_____

_____

_____

_____

_____

9. When your weight is up or down, does it affect your self confidence? How? Why?

_____

_____

_____

_____

_____

_____

_____

_____

_____

_____

_____

_____

_____

10. Do you find yourself attractive when you look in the mirror? Are you comparing yourself to an unattainable image of perfection? Can you adjust your mindset to feel truly sexy as you are? (If the answer is no, we need to address this.)

11. Does your partner comment on your body positively or negatively? Do you make similar comments?

DIET

People hate going on diets!

Human nature is incentive based. It refuses to change if that change provides less enjoyment or causes more distress than the current situation.

Creating a clear understanding of our incentives will help us accept short term discomforts.

In reality weight gain preoccupation affects intimacy.

Apart from the possible loss of attraction from one or both partners, weight gain negatively impacts energy, has long term health risks and can be a real drag on your self image.

Here are a few suggestions that when followed will yield results within days.

When To Eat
Break the Day Down to 3- 8 Hour Cycles

Intake 12pm-8pm
Assimilation 8pm-4am
Elimination 4am-12pm

If you choose to stay on this diet long-term, you will inevitably reach a plateau. A plateau is when the body withholds weight loss because your exercise or work load exceeds the fat storage and the body senses death. The body remains committed to your survival and withholds calories by creating exhaustion so that you minimize your energy expenditure. You need only to keep going. This is a war. Eventually a breakthrough will occur and the weight loss will resume.

What To Eat

Elimination Cycle:
Only food high in water content is allowed. Water, Tea, Coffee, Vegetables, Fruit. The use of olive oil, seasonings, salt and pepper are permitted.

Intake Cycle:
Choose a protein and a vegetable for the greatest yield for weight loss.

Begin with NO SUGAR or starch. Starch breaks down into sugar and the body uses it for immediate fuel, canceling out the whole process.

Protein and starch cannot be eaten together.

Drink before your meals not during. Water that is consumed during a meal will bloat the system and slow digestion.

Fruit cannot be eaten before or after a meal for 3 hours as it creates butane gas.

Use fruits only during the elimination cycle.

Nuts and seeds are acceptable at all times.

If for some reason you do go off the diet, just go back on the next day, no drama. So you blew it, keep going. You'll see the damage corrected in a day or two. Weigh yourself in the morning only.

Good Luck!!

Sarah Fraser

CHAPTER 5

FAMILY

Family is the MOST IMPORTANT thing. Being open, flexible, and trying to truly understand each other's perspective when approaching the topic of family will create genuine understanding. Family means different things to different people and how ever you and your partner decide to define this is up to you. What's most important is that you talk about what family means and what each of you expects. Discussing your views on children, how many you would like, and when the time is right, is the first step in imagining your ideal family structure. The primary relationship in any family is the couple. Children's needs and demands deserve every bit of attention you can give. This need not be at the expense of your relationship. In a perfect world, the children grow up and leave. If you haven't maintained intimacy and connection with one another, the relationship will be lacking. The greatest legacy you can leave your children is the example of a loving relationship between parents. It is the foundation they will build on forever.

QUESTIONS ON FAMILY

1. What are your core child rearing philosophies, styles and techniques? Will you set a time schedule vs baby demand?
2. Discipline styles: physical vs verbal? Reward vs punishment? How were you disciplined as a child?
3. How will having a child affect your lifestyle? Sleep hours, work hours, spontaneity, free time? Dinner time? Smoking, alcohol use?
4. What do you need to change in your environment to create a healthier living space? Safety, air quality?
5. What are your feelings about genetic testing during pregnancy?
6. Describe how you picture your everyday routine as a parent. Changing diapers, feeding, playing, cleaning, juggling work, car pooling, bathing? List three ideals you would like to prioritize as part of your family routine. Nightly family dinners, a day of the week off for each of you, date night?
7. What other families do you admire? How would you like your family to emulate them? Do you have friends with families that share your common interests?
8. What are some things you liked about the way you were raised and what would you like to do differently as a parent?
9. What will the division of labor be? Do we automatically assume the woman will take all ownership of household and children duties and the man will earn all of the money

10. What are the expectations around intimacy after children?

11. Do we have a will? A trust? Do you think these are just for older couples?

12. If we mutually decide for one person to be a full-time caregiver, does that have value? How much value? For how long?

13. How might you encourage or discourage your in-laws' participation in your parenting? Are we aligned in how to navigate uncomfortable situations as they arise?

14. What is the timeline you have in mind for having children (a certain age, time span, etc.)? Are there things you want to accomplish first? Please consult your Rav

15. Which of your qualities are best suited for parenting? Which do you feel needs improvement

16. What do you anticipate as the biggest challenge in parenting? Do you know how to apologize? To your spouse? Do children deserve apologies?

17. How do you feel about birth control?

18. What kind of legacy do you want our marriage to reflect? Are we practicing those values now? Will they be successfully passed to the next generation?

1. What are your core child rearing philosophies, styles and techniques? Will you set a time schedule vs baby demand?

_____

_____

_____

_____

_____

_____

_____

_____

_____

_____

_____

_____

2. Discipline styles: physical vs verbal? Reward vs punishment? How were you disciplined as a child?

3. How will having a child affect your lifestyle? Sleep hours, work hours, spontaneity, free time? Dinner time? Smoking, alcohol use?

_____

_____

_____

_____

_____

_____

_____

_____

_____

_____

_____

_____

_____

4. What do you need to change in your environment to create a healthier living space? Safety, air quality?

_____

_____

_____

_____

_____

_____

_____

_____

_____

_____

_____

_____

_____

5.What are your feelings about genetic testing during pregnancy?

_____

_____

_____

_____

_____

_____

_____

_____

_____

_____

_____

_____

_____

6. Describe how you picture your everyday routine as a parent. Changing diapers, feeding, playing, cleaning, juggling work, car pooling, bathing? List three ideals you would like to prioritize as part of your family routine. Nightly family dinners, a day of the week off for each of you, date night?

7.What other families do you admire? How would you like your family to emulate them? Do you have friends with families that share your common interests?

8. What are some things you liked about the way you were raised and what would you like to do differently as a parent?

_____

_____

_____

_____

_____

_____

_____

_____

_____

_____

_____

_____

_____

9.What will the division of labor be? Do we automatically assume the woman will take all ownership of household and children duties and the man will earn all of the money?

_____

_____

_____

_____

_____

_____

_____

_____

_____

_____

_____

_____

_____

10. What are the expectations around intimacy after children?

_____

_____

_____

_____

_____

_____

_____

_____

_____

_____

_____

_____

_____

11. Do we have a will? A trust? Do you think these are just for older couples?

_____

_____

_____

_____

_____

_____

_____

_____

_____

_____

_____

_____

_____

12. If we mutually decide for one person to be a full-time caregiver, does that have value? How much value? For how long?

13.How might you encourage or discourage your in-laws' participation in your parenting? Are we aligned in how to navigate uncomfortable situations as they arise?

_____

_____

_____

_____

_____

_____

_____

_____

_____

_____

_____

_____

_____

14. What is the timeline you have in mind for having children (a certain age, time span, etc.)? Are there things you want to accomplish first? Please consult your Rav

---

---

15. Which of your qualities are best suited for parenting? Which do you feel needs improvement?

_____

_____

_____

_____

_____

_____

_____

_____

_____

_____

_____

_____

_____

16. What do you anticipate as the biggest challenge in parenting? Do you know how to apologize? To your spouse? Do children deserve apologies?

17. How do you feel about birth control?

18. What kind of legacy do you want our marriage to reflect? Are we practicing those values now? Will they be successfully passed to the next generation?

FAMILY

It is important for a couple to discuss how and when to start a family without causing anger or disappointment. It is advisable to consult with your Rav if one of you feels unprepared to begin a family right away. Before discussing specifics both partners need to acknowledge that it is a very personal conversation and commit to a respectful dialogue. Accept that it is not just one person's decision to make and recognize that it will be a collaborative effort. Neither partner should feel that the responsibility lies solely on them. It can be helpful to create a joint timeline of family decisions founded on an actual agreement. Talk openly about fears and discuss the impact of any proposed path forward. Another subject to consider around family dynamics is the participation of extended family. When it comes to living in harmony with in-laws or siblings, there is a lot of pressure put on couples. The first step to maintaining peace is to establish boundaries. This means that limits need to be set between the couple and family members in order to ensure appropriate behavior and privacy. Couples should also agree on communication methods and what topics are acceptable to discuss with whom. These boundaries need to be kept consistent if they are going to be effective in helping couples coexist with extended family.

What to do when children pick up bad habits or values from family members? The family has a powerful influence on the lives of children. Children learn by observing the behavior of those around them and by imitating their parents, siblings, and other close family members. Unfortunately this means that if bad habits are modeled, the kids may imitate them and incorporate them into their own behavior. When children pick up bad habits, it can be a challenge to address. However it is important to do so, as this behavior can have a negative impact on the child's development and on the family as a whole. The first step is to identify the underlying cause of the behavior which could range from peer pressure to poor parental role modeling. Once the root cause is determined, the next step is to find ways to firmly address the issue and keep a focus on the health and safety of the child first and foremost. Different parenting styles can cause a lot of trouble. When this occurs a date night is in order. A long intimate conversation alone with a glass of wine (or two) can help the couple sort out their feelings, and create a united front. Actively listening to your partner's perception is key in being able to resolve the problem.

Sarah Fraser

CHAPTER 6

FINANCES

Money is one of the main reasons couples fight. Whether poor or rich, money can be a source of great conflict in a relationship. Time, money and work are issues that permeate every marriage. The time to uncover our similarities and differences is before the issues grow into insurmountable problems. Different perceptions about what it means to be financially stable are common. What is important is how a couple handles their financial disagreements. Work can take up as much time and energy as our relationship itself. Having open conversations about our commitment to our work is just as important as the conversations around our commitment to marriage. Both commitments demand our time and attention. Finding a way to satisfy both is vital to the success of the relationship.

QUESTIONS ON MONEY

1. What do you think about money? Can money buy happiness?
2. What did your parents prioritize spending their money on? Did they fight about expenditures?
3. How do you spend your money? Do you feel guilty buying something for yourself?
4. How much do you earn? Is it enough?
5. How much do you save? For what purpose?
6. What is the best use of money?
7. How does money affect your happiness? Are your moods controlled by your finances?
8. How do you define rich or wealthy? How do you feel about these people?
9. What do you think about people who have less than they need? Do you give charity? How do you choose who to give to?
10. How much money do you want to make in this lifetime? How much money do you need to retire? Is someone advising you financially?
11. Are we in debt? How do we address this?
12. Is one person financially dependent on the other? If you are the one at home, do you feel your contribution to the household is valued?
13. Who decides how to spend money and on what? Does this lead to arguments?
14. Do you justify long hours at work so as to avoid the evening routine? Are you hiding out at work?
15. What are your thoughts about your partner's absence?

1. What do you think about money? Can money buy happiness?

_____

_____

_____

_____

_____

_____

_____

_____

_____

_____

_____

_____

_____

2. What did your parents prioritize spending their money on? Did they fight about expenditures?

_____

_____

_____

_____

_____

_____

_____

_____

_____

_____

_____

_____

_____

3. How do you spend your money? Do you feel guilty buying something for yourself?

4. How much do you earn? Is it enough?

_____

_____

_____

_____

_____

_____

_____

_____

_____

_____

_____

_____

_____

5. How much do you save? For what purpose?

6. What is the best use of money?

_____

_____

_____

_____

_____

_____

_____

_____

_____

_____

_____

_____

_____

7. How does money affect your happiness? Are your moods controlled by your finances?

_____

_____

_____

_____

_____

_____

_____

_____

_____

_____

_____

_____

_____

_____

8. How do you define rich or wealthy? How do you feel about these people?

_____

_____

_____

_____

_____

_____

_____

_____

_____

_____

_____

_____

_____

9. What do you think about people who have less than they need? Do you give charity? How do you choose who to give to?

---

10. How much money do you want to make in this lifetime? How much money do you need to retire? Is someone advising you financially?

_____

_____

_____

_____

_____

_____

_____

_____

_____

_____

_____

_____

_____

11. Are we in debt? How do we address this?

12. Is one person financially dependent on the other? If you are the one at home, do you feel your contribution to the household is valued?

13. Who decides how to spend money and on what? Does this lead to arguments?

_____

_____

_____

_____

_____

_____

_____

_____

_____

_____

_____

_____

_____

14. Do you justify long hours at work so as to avoid the evening routine? Are you hiding out at work?

_____

_____

_____

_____

_____

_____

_____

_____

_____

_____

_____

_____

15. What are your thoughts about your partner's absence?

_____

_____

_____

_____

_____

_____

_____

_____

_____

_____

_____

_____

NOTES

$ MONEY $

In today's world finances are a common reason for couples arguing as money is a finite commodity. It is important that couples agree on how it will be managed and distributed. Conflict over finances can be emotionally and mentally draining and it is important to learn how to resolve such matters in a peaceful manner. The following are some tips that couples can employ to productively and peacefully resolve financial issues.

The first and most important step to take is to have open and honest communication on the issue. The key to successful resolution is to have both partners on the same page, and able to express all concerns, ideas, worries, and expectations. Each spouse must be conscious not to berate their partner or make them feel guilty due to the financial issue. This can create further resentment and anger which is counter productive.

Another way to come to a peaceful resolution over finances is for couples to create a budget together and stick to it. Establishing a plan for how money is going to be earned and how it's going to be spent can alleviate any conflict or disagreement on how money is prioritized. Utilizing a spread sheet or computer program to record spending can help keep both partners honest and transparent about their financial activities. There are many new and innovative ways to save such as; "No spend weeks", opening a savings account and setting up an auto transfer after your paychecks get deposited, shopping at discount stores, etc.

- Create a budget and stick to it. This will help people identify their financial priorities and determine how much money to allocate towards necessary items/activities and how much to save.
- Take advantage of rewards programs. Many banks, stores and credit card companies offer rewards programs that can help couples save money through discounts of points that can be redeemed for valuable items or services.
- Make use of coupons. Coupons are a great way to save money on necessary items. Consider cheaper alternatives. Consider options for services such as investing in a shared streaming service like Netflix.
- Ask friends for advice on less expensive options for furniture and appliances. Research large purchases in advance and search for the best price.
- Cook at home instead of eating out. Huge savings can be had by meal prepping lunches for work and always having your coffee at home as opposed to buying from a shop.
- Shop around for the best deals. Compare prices online and in stores to get the best deal possible.
- Use cash instead of credit cards. Paying with cash eliminates the temptation to overspend and can help the couple stick to their budget.
- Travel during off peak periods. Rates are less expensive during off peak times and couples can save a great deal of money.
- Take advantage of free entertainment. Visit local parks or museums with free admission days or watch a movie at a friend's house.
- Save on utility bills. Make sure to turn off the lights.

Make saving money a priority. Save 10-15% of your income for retirement and other major life expenses. Couples can allocate money in a variety of savings vehicles. Ask a professional about opening a 401K or IRA account, bank account, or any number of real estate investments. Spending wisely means setting realistic budgets that include expenses for both present and long-term needs. This will help to avoid debt accumulation over time. Increasing income creatively with side hustles can boost future financial security. Seeking new sources of additional income will help the ability to save each month. Ensure that you have adequate insurance policies such as life, health and disability to protect your financial wellbeing. Always reassess the budget when one or the other starts making more or less money. It is important to reassess and adapt to any changes in income. This helps to provide financial clarity on financial decisions and expectations in the relationship. Re-evaluate the situation on a regular basis to determine if an adjustment could be made to alleviate stress, like finding a more affordable living situation. It is important to recognize each party's contribution to the relationship regardless of income disparity. Taking time to show appreciation is essential for both parties to continue to do their best. Reach out to family and friends for help like babysitting, transportation or emotional support. Finding creative solutions if one partner is unable to work such as part time employment, a work from home job or freelancing. Sharing responsibilities like household chores and parenting is an important part of the function of the relationship and stress management. Nurture the relationship in spite of the stress and remember to nurture yourself. Spend quality time together and create healthy ways to cope with additional demands.

Sarah Fraser

CHAPTER 7

MAKING MEMORIES

Gd gave us life to enjoy. A successful couple can have similar interests or not. The most important thing is to respect each other's ideas of fun. One partner may think an ATV ride through the jungle is exhilarating while the other wants to relax on the beach all day. It's all good fun! Find commonalities and enjoy them together while supporting your partner in their own idea of enjoyment and adventure. The fun goes out of many marriages when children and work begin to overwhelm the relationship. Make a concerted effort to keep fun alive. Supporting connection, reinforcing laughter and positive bonding will make the marriage thrive. As they say, "Laughter is the best medicine."

QUESTIONS ON ENJOYMENT

1. What does play/ adventure mean to you? Have you forgotten how to play?
2. How did you like to play when you were a child? Did you play alone or with friends? Were they friends or rivals?
3. What's the most fun you've had in the last few years? Do these memories lift your spirits when you're down?
4. What places are on your bucket list? What do you want out of these experiences? Do you envision having these experiences alone?
5. How do you think we could have more fun? What part do you play?
6. When was the last time we did something new together? What was it? Who planned it?
7. What's a day-long adventure we could have together? Where should we go? What should we do?
8. Do you enjoy seeing your partner have fun

Couples Who
PLAY TOGETHER
STAY TOGETHER

1. What does play/ adventure mean to you?
Have you forgotten how to play?

_____

_____

_____

_____

_____

_____

_____

_____

_____

_____

_____

_____

_____

2. How did you like to play when you were a child? Did you play alone or with friends? Were they friends or rivals?

_____

_____

_____

_____

_____

_____

_____

_____

_____

_____

_____

_____

_____

3. What's the most fun you've had in the last few years? Do these memories lift your spirits when you're down?

_____

_____

_____

_____

_____

_____

_____

_____

_____

_____

_____

_____

_____

4. What places are on your bucket list? What do you want out of these experiences? Do you envision having these experiences alone?

_____

_____

_____

_____

_____

_____

_____

_____

_____

_____

_____

_____

_____

5. How do you think we could have more fun? What part do you play?

_____

_____

_____

_____

_____

_____

_____

_____

_____

_____

_____

_____

_____

6. When was the last time we did something new together? What was it? Who planned it?

_____

_____

_____

_____

_____

_____

_____

_____

_____

_____

_____

_____

_____

7. What's a day-long adventure we could have together? Where should we go? What should we do?

_____

_____

_____

_____

_____

_____

_____

_____

_____

_____

_____

_____

_____

8. Do you enjoy seeing your partner have fun?

_____

_____

_____

_____

_____

_____

_____

_____

_____

_____

_____

_____

_____

NOTES

LET'S ENJOY EACH OTHER

Hiking is an outdoor activity couples can participate in together. Hiking adventures are especially meaningful for couples because it is something that can take up a lot of time. It is a chance for fresh air and a nice experience. Hiking can be done on easier beginner levels and couples can work their way up from there depending on the level of intensity they are comfortable with. If nature walks such as hiking through the forest, walking along the beach or other kinds of trails are not easily accessible, you can always go for walks around your neighborhood or even the local shopping mall. This can be a suitable alternative for bad weather to just get out of the house.

Kayaking and canoeing are another enjoyable activity that couples can do together to experience the great outdoors. It's also a great way to bond over the activity and learn a new skill that can be useful in other adventure experiences. Kayaking and canoeing can also be made more interesting by taking different routes and visiting new destinations.

Camping is extremely affordable and there are endless possibilities.

Outdoor adventures can be some of the most rewarding experiences couples can enjoy together. Unfortunately, fun is often overlooked because of other concerns being prioritized. It is important to create meaningful memories to share and remember.

Cooking classes are also a great way to learn something new together and the new found skill can be used to spice up mealtime. Taking any type of class together, be it a pottery class, language class or wine tasting for example, can create new memories for the couple to share and can give them a chance to bond over something outside of their routine lives.

Traveling is another way for couples to add some real adventure and fun into their marriage. Taking a local, national or international vacation can spark new conversations and experiences. Word to the wise; book with a reputable travel agent and save yourselves the stress of planning.

If you like board games, they can be an affordable and fun way to play together with friends or for date nights at home.

For the artistic couples, you can go to a paint night together or buy supplies and do it yourself at home. There are many youtube videos for instructions.

You can also turn up the music and DANCE!
Dancing is not only fun but also great for intimacy as you need to be in tune to each other's moves, so you don't step on each other's toes!

144

Sarah Fraser

CHAPTER 8

SELF-IMAGE & CONFIDENCE

Truth always stands in the world. When something is true
for you, you are motivated to follow through. It's when other
opinions don't match your truth, you get confused.
People pleasing creates unhappy people. For example;
going on a diet for someone else isn't sustainable.
How you see yourself is how you talk to yourself; make good
friends with this idea. You can take control of the force
inside of you that is feeding you negative ideas. Self-
confidence comes from your own awareness of this force
and deciding not to listen but proceed nonetheless.
Indulging in insecurities is your brain's way of avoiding
change and keeping you safe.
Self- confidence is often confused with confidence.
Confidence however is based on evidence from one's past.
We look to our past experiences, knowledge and abilities to
know we can take on a particular task. Confidence is based
on a belief system that has evidence.

I have a secret for you. Your self-image and self-confidence has nothing to do with your body.

Bodies change with age, especially after children, a crisis or a significant life change (for women AND men). You will not feel the same when you look in the mirror at 40 as you did at 25. It's all about your thoughts and what you believe about yourself. There are sexy and self-confident people of all sizes and shapes. Your self-confidence comes from identifying and living in your purpose and re-wiring negative thought patterns through changing your belief system. You and you alone, are in control of your body and mind. When you realize no one can take self-confidence away from you with an unkind word or look, you can begin to stand in your own power. That kind of confidence is radiant and you guessed it- attractive. What do you think when you look in the mirror?

the secrets of jewish women

QUESTIONS ON CONFIDENCE

1. What habits and skills have you cultivated over the years that enabled your personal development?
2. Have you persevered after failure? Did you eventually succeed?
3. If you fail to achieve a goal, do you keep trying? How do you view that failure? Do you learn from it?
4. How do you talk yourself into and out of new situations?
5. Do you have a role model that you admire? Is it their confidence or self-confidence that you are attracted to?
6. Would you volunteer yourself for a new and seemingly scary experience and be able to risk failure?
7. Why is it important to understand the difference between confidence and self-confidence?
8. How does one cultivate self-confidence?
9. What causes a person to lose confidence ? What is lack of self-confidence?
10. Do insecurities create a lack of confidence or self-confidence? How?

Your self-confidence ultimately comes from your opinion about yourself.
You are in control. Don't let anyone else define you.

1. What habits and skills have you cultivated over the years that enabled your personal development?

---

2. Have you persevered after failure?
Did you eventually succeed?

_____

_____

_____

_____

_____

_____

_____

_____

_____

_____

_____

_____

_____

3. If you fail to achieve a goal, do you keep trying? How do you view that failure? Do you learn from it?

---

4. How do you talk yourself into and out of new situations?

---

5. Do you have a role model that you admire? Is it their confidence or self-confidence that you are attracted to?

_____

_____

_____

_____

_____

_____

_____

_____

_____

_____

_____

_____

_____

6. Would you volunteer yourself for a new and seemingly scary experience and be able to risk failure?

7. Why is it important to understand the difference between confidence and self-confidence?

_____

_____

_____

_____

_____

_____

_____

_____

_____

_____

_____

_____

_____

8. How does one cultivate self-confidence?

_____

_____

_____

_____

_____

_____

_____

_____

_____

_____

_____

_____

_____

**9. What causes a person to lose confidence?
What is lack of self-confidence?**

_____

_____

_____

_____

_____

_____

_____

_____

_____

_____

_____

_____

_____

10. Do insecurities create a lack of confidence or self-confidence? How?

NOTES

A WOMANS SELF-IMAGE

SOCIETAL PRESSURE   *Men's Tips*

Many women are taught from a very young age that their worth is somehow tied up in their beauty. Women are praised or ignored for how they look. They are fed millions of images of what "real" beauty is and how they fall short. This takes a toll over time. While it is completely untrue that a woman's value lies only in her appearance, this concept is so deeply embedded in her psyche that we have to work with it. Oftentimes a woman is unable to separate her character values of kindness - nurturing - loving, and hardworking from her looks. She is constantly comparing herself to the "ideal" image of beauty that she herself lacks.

WHAT TO DO ABOUT IT

Compliment her often. When she asks for your opinion about her appearance, the only answer is: "You look beautiful in everything". Remember that her own discomfort with herself is the result of her insecurities. Not a personal rejection of you. Read that again.

If she's uncomfortable, do everything in your power to convince her of your desire and attraction. It will sink in. Celebrate the inevitable body changes that occur over time. She is perfect no matter what. Perceive her as she is, the vessel for light and love for your family.

Small daily affirmations from the only man who matters in her life will go a long way in repairing the damage society has done to her self image. When she truly believes that you see her, all of her, and find her beautiful, she will open up like a flower forever in bloom.

159

SELF-CONFIDENCE

Your ability to believe in yourself without any evidence or history around the thing you are about to undertake, is generated internally and is at the core of self-confidence. Self-confidence is the emotion of growth which propels us forward. When we are self-confident we go after new endeavors and take risks regardless of our past failures.

Self-confidence is the willingness to feel any emotion from loss to humiliation or fear. When we are self-confident, we are sure that emotions are momentary and will pass. When you are prepared to feel anything, you are developing the self-confidence necessary to move forward in life.

Ask yourself, "What am I afraid to feel?" Become willing to get friendly with uncomfortable emotions. Build up self-confidence by having your own back. What does this mean? It means that when you make mistakes you don't beat yourself up with destructive self-talk. You lean in and move forward.

Being too reliant on confidence means that you will only attempt what you have done before. You will never grow. Cultivating self-confidence however will open up endless doors of new possibility.

HOW TO...

- Practice awareness of your thoughts, recognize what you are thinking. Do these thoughts serve my purpose? If not, understand you are in control, stop thinking this way.
- What do I want to think? Think conscious and deliberate thoughts that will take you where you want to go. Keep your focus on the future, the other thoughts will weaken.
- Develop a positive affirmation practice. Look in the mirror. Say nice things to yourself. Smile.
- Make a list of your best qualities.
- Spend time alone reflecting on your relationship with Gd. Are you able to verbally speak to Gd? Who else do you think will help you?
- Engage with hobbies that make you feel joy. Be creative, try new things.
- Do not limit or avoid activities that make you feel self-conscious or down, do them anyway.

CHANGING THINKING PATTERNS

Thinking I am unworthy, ugly or unprepared is counterproductive.
Instead: Think I am worthy, I am beautiful and prepared, I can do this. Give yourself a wink in the mirror. Only you can do this work, no one can do this for you.

Always attach an action to the thought. This is critical to changing the unwanted mindset. Thoughts remain in the spiritual realm until they are physically actualized.

Failure means that you've taken action. You have failed forward. This is the way life works. This is a universal law that any action moves you forward. Your thoughts create direction which you then act upon. If you don't like where you're moving, you must first change the thought, that will change the feeling, then you can change the action and ultimately your direction.

We are all moving forward no matter what. If you feel like you are not moving forward it is actually a product of blocked thought patterns.

There are two action steps you can take to help rewire the brain when you are experiencing conflicting thoughts.

The first method is best used when dealing with unpleasant thoughts relating to difficult circumstances like grief or loss. This entails writing down every thought as you are thinking it. By filling up a whole sheet of paper you are draining the brain of these thoughts. When they are all out, throw the paper away.
DO NOT RE-READ THIS.
The purpose of this exercise is to take the thoughts out and put them into a physical state. We do not want to reinforce these negative or damaging thoughts by re-reading them and reintroducing the ideas back into our subconscious.

The second method is best used when we are aware that our thoughts are not serving us and we need to improve them and take on a new behavior. This method is not the same as the above.
We reread and change the negative statements into a positive statement; and add an actionable and doable step.

We change the negative thoughts into positive mantras that motivate us to take action.

The goal is to become aware of our thoughts and disable the negative behavior by rewiring new thought patterns.

Sarah Fraser

CHAPTER 9

DREAMS

Dreams are how we grow our lives. Big dreams hold big magic. Big dreams need not be limited to large homes and lavish cars. Concepts like a long lasting and loving marriage, a warm family full of support, a wholesome home, good health and happiness are values to cultivate.

Dreaming together is a profound act and honoring each other's dreams is a way to express deep love for your partner.

When two people are aligned with one dream, they can move mountains.

QUESTIONS ON DREAMS

1. What were your dreams for yourself as a child? Have you realized any of them? Were they your dreams or your family's expectations? Did you chase those expectations and do things that didn't feel right for you?
2. Is there such a thing as too many big dreams? Why? Do you find yourself dreaming with no action? Why?
3. If you fail to achieve a dream, do you keep trying? How do you view that failure? Do you learn from it?
4. How do we plan as a couple to execute our shared dreams? Who does what?
5. What are you doing today to pursue your dreams? Have you practically analyzed your dreams? Do you know how?
6. How can I participate in your dreams? Do your dreams involve us?
7. Where do you feel most inspired?
8. What is a passion we share that we can pursue together?
9. What is the most meaningful thing we have accomplished together?
10. What else would you like to accomplish together? Do you believe we can?

1. What were your dreams for yourself as a child? Have you realized any of them? Were they your dreams or your family's expectations? Did you chase those expectations and do things that didn't feel right for you?

_____

_____

_____

_____

_____

_____

_____

_____

_____

_____

_____

_____

_____

_____

2. Is there such a thing as too many big dreams? Why? Do you find yourself dreaming with no action? Why?

_____

_____

_____

_____

_____

_____

_____

_____

_____

_____

_____

_____

_____

_____

3. If you fail to achieve a dream, do you keep trying? How do you view that failure? Do you learn from it?

---

4. How do we plan as a couple to execute our shared dreams? Who does what?

_____

_____

_____

_____

_____

_____

_____

_____

_____

_____

_____

_____

5. What are you doing today to pursue your dreams? Have you practically analyzed your dreams? Do you know how?

6. How can I participate in your dreams? Do your dreams involve us?

_____

_____

_____

_____

_____

_____

_____

_____

_____

_____

_____

_____

_____

_____

7. Where do you feel most inspired?

8. What is a passion we share that we can pursue together?

_____

_____

_____

_____

_____

_____

_____

_____

_____

_____

_____

_____

_____

9. What is the most meaningful thing we have accomplished together?

_____

_____

_____

_____

_____

_____

_____

_____

_____

_____

_____

_____

10. What else would you like to accomplish together? Do you believe we can?

_____

_____

_____

_____

_____

_____

_____

_____

_____

_____

_____

_____

NOTES

DREAMS

Dreams and fantasy are sometimes used interchangeably. Dreams are one of the most powerful and fascinating aspects of the human experience. Being a source of mystery and intrigue for centuries, theorists and researchers have been trying to unlock the hidden meaning behind them. To this day, scientists are still trying to decipher the age-old question "what do dreams really mean?"

There is no simple answer to this question as every individual's dreams are unique and personal. Dreams reflect a person's thoughts and feelings as well as provide a glimpse into the future. People process the events of their day while dreaming and this can act as a coping mechanism for difficult times. Sometimes they can also provide hope, giving an individual a sense of clarity, direction or purpose.

Fantasy on the other hand is conscious imagination, tending to focus on ideas and situations that are either possible or highly likely. Fantasies are often used as a way to escape reality or to imagine a better one. Dreaming is an unconscious process of having imaginary experiences while sleeping. They are symbolic, stemming randomly from experiences in one's life and are often perceived as being unexplainable. Dreaming can help in visualizing a path for the future by allowing one to tap into their subconscious. Dreams can be seen as a reflection of our inner thoughts, desires and fears.

When one takes the time to process symbolic messages they can gain insight into their own motivations. Retrieving unresolved issues that remain in memory is a way to use dreams to unblock one's obstacles. By reflecting on dreams we can better understand ourselves, form better action plans and make decisions that will help steer our future in the desired direction.

People often confuse other people in their dreams as a reality.

A tip for analyzing your dreams: Replace the people and objects with yourself. Sometimes these people are familiar, which can be confusing. By not getting sidetracked by other people or objects presented in your dream, you can gain more insight into what's troubling you. Lay for a moment before getting up reviewing the events of the dream using this perspective. Everything and everyone is a reflection of you.
Give it a try.

FANTASY

Love requires no explanation. It is the most pure and powerful emotion that one can feel. No wonder we fantasize about the one we love. It is because they are the primary object of our affections, so naturally our thoughts turn to them. Could there be something deeper and more complex at play? The power of fantasy can be incredibly powerful and it is our thoughts, ideas, desires and dreams that shape reality. We often take our need for attention and release and use fantasy for emotional gratification. We can envision our perfect relationship, self, and use those fantasy interpretations to stir the emotional connection of love in our minds. This act allows us to temporarily feel the presence of the one we adore and because we are innately creative, we can craft, create and design our perfect scenarios. Fantasy also allows us to explore concepts which can sometimes be too much for reality. They allow us to envision scenarios that make us feel complete and fulfilled. We can grow our understanding with different possibilities without repercussions and travel a world of limitless possibilities. It cannot be denied that exploring the depths of an emotion can be something both exhilarating but also intimidating. Fantasy moves us away from reality and allows us to feel the bliss brought about by love and safety without the fear of rejection. Plan date nights. Take time planning date nights for each other. This shows that you value your partner's needs and can help keep intimacy alive. Imagine creative adventures that you can do together to keep things romantic. This could be dinner out once a week, watching your favorite show together or setting aside time to just reconnect in different ways. Visualize different scenarios and take actionable steps to spice things up.Get into a comfortable position and close your eyes.

Reach back into your memory. Think about when you and your partner first met and were in the infatuation stage. Revisit the earliest moments of excitement and feel your heartbeat, your hands shake, the spark. Let yourself lose track of time. Remember how good you felt about yourself, how vulnerable and secure you were able to be. Feel that. Then go into the bedroom!

This will certainly help you look forward to being together with your partner.Your bedroom needs to be a private retreat for you and your partner. Make your bedroom aesthetically pleasing to the senses with things like candles, nice sheets, dark curtains and a pleasant scent.

Sarah Fraser

CHAPTER 10

GROWTH & SPIRITUALITY

The only thing that's constant in this lifetime is change. You will grow and evolve and your partner will too. Your ability as a couple to welcome and support each other's growth will lead to less resistance and more love in your marriage. The trick is, not to fall in love with your *idea* of your partner or your *idea* of what that person could be. Love the person in front of you, every day, no matter what. The purpose of marriage is to unite with someone you love for the rest of your life. Time and again we've heard from couples that Niddah didn't work for them and led to arguments, so they gave up. A common complaint is that Taharat Mishpacha lessons leave many gaps regarding sexual behavior.

Keeping Nidah is about transcending each other's physical forms, which enables you to find yourselves in each other. A preoccupation with physical form has the opposite effect. Both parties will end up lost in superficiality. Remember, marriage is understood to mean that the husband and wife are merging into a single soul. A man is considered "incomplete" if he is not married, as his soul is one part of a larger whole that remains to be unified in marriage.

"You are created to have a relationship with Gd. You are not here to make a great name for yourself. You are here to know Gd."

QUESTIONS ON SPIRITUALITY

1. What goals do we have in life? For ourselves personally and as a couple?
2. What is the role of religion in our lives? What was its role in our families growing up? What would you keep or change?
3. What do you consider sacred? Why?
4. What carries us through difficult times?
5. What is your source of peace?
6. What religious beliefs and practices do we want to pass down to our children? Why?
7. How do you feel about personal development and growth? How do you seek your own growth? Do you define growth as simply physical? Do you feel the need to grow spiritually?
8. What is prayer to you? When do you pray? Is your relationship with Gd a priority?
9. Do you view physical intimacy as a spiritual experience? Explain.
10. Can you think of a time that you were struggling with something, did you turn to a Rav (or want to) for guidance?
11. How much or how little formal Jewish education would we want for our children?

1. What goals do we have in life? For ourselves personally and as a couple?

_____

_____

_____

_____

_____

_____

_____

_____

_____

_____

_____

_____

_____

_____

2. What is the role of religion in our lives? What was its role in our families growing up? What would you keep or change?

3. What do you consider sacred? Why?

4. What carries us through difficult times?

_____

_____

_____

_____

_____

_____

_____

_____

_____

_____

_____

_____

_____

_____

5. What is your source of peace?

_____

_____

_____

_____

_____

_____

_____

_____

_____

_____

_____

_____

_____

6. What religious beliefs and practices do we want to pass down to our children? Why?

_____

_____

_____

_____

_____

_____

_____

_____

_____

_____

_____

_____

_____

7. How do you feel about personal development and growth? How do you seek your own growth? Do you define growth as simply physical? Do you feel the need to grow spiritually?

_____

_____

_____

_____

_____

_____

_____

_____

_____

_____

_____

_____

8. What is prayer to you? When do you pray? Is your relationship with Gd a priority?

_____

_____

_____

_____

_____

_____

_____

_____

_____

_____

_____

_____

_____

9. Do you view physical intimacy as a spiritual experience? Explain.

10. Can you think of a time that you were struggling with something, did you turn to a Rav (or want to) for guidance?

_____

_____

_____

_____

_____

_____

_____

_____

_____

_____

_____

_____

_____

11. How much or how little formal Jewish education would we want for our children?

_____

_____

_____

_____

_____

_____

_____

_____

_____

_____

_____

_____

NOTES

Sarah Fraser

CHAPTER 11

SEX & INTIMACY

We all want passionate and connected relationships. It's unrealistic to think that sex will always be deeply romantic. Usually, women need to feel emotionally connected to have sex, and men need to have sex to feel emotionally connected. Most importantly, sex should never become another burden at the end of the day. Lighten the mood by becoming more playful. Intimacy starts outside of the bedroom with small gestures such as saying "I love you" often, and meaning it. Complimenting your partner, kissing one another passionately, and frequent touches when walking past all lead up to genuine intimacy. It's important to be open to your partners' different sexual preferences. Learn how to emotionally connect so you can create powerful bonds in and out of the bedroom.

Let's talk about SEX.

the secrets of jewish women

**Great sex is vital for both men and women.
We were created to have sexual fulfillment in our marriages.**

the secrets of jewish women

QUESTIONS ON SEX

1. How often during the day do you think about having sex?
2. How do you prepare? Do you fantasize? Are you open to experimenting?
3. What is your goal for sex? Do you think it is the same for your partner?
4. What turns you on? Are you comfortable asking your partner to meet your needs? Are you embarrassed to ask?
5. How and where do you like to be touched? Do you even know?
6. Do you feel comfortable asking your partner these questions?
7. Do you or your partner have a special way to ask for sex?
8. What happens when one person is too tired or disengaged?
9. How do you deal with this reaction?
10. Have you noticed if you and your partner have a favorite position? Have you discussed this with each other?
11. What is your favorite time to make love? Are you open to spontaneity?
12. How often would you like to have sex? When? Where?
13. Do you ensure you are both satisfied?
14. Is there anything sexually you would like to try? What can we do to make our sex life better? Can you tell me? Can I tell you?
15. Is there a focus during sex on imperfect body image? Are we able to focus on what we do like about ourselves and each other?
16. Do you avoid touching yourself in a personal way? Why?
17. How can we make our bedroom into a place to play?

1. How often during the day do you think about having sex?

_____

_____

_____

_____

_____

_____

_____

_____

_____

_____

_____

_____

2. How do you prepare? Do you fantasize? Are you open to experimenting?

_____

_____

_____

_____

_____

_____

_____

_____

_____

_____

_____

_____

_____

_____

3. What is your goal for sex? Do you think it is the same for your partner?

_____

_____

_____

_____

_____

_____

_____

_____

_____

_____

_____

_____

_____

4. What turns you on? Are you comfortable asking your partner to meet your needs? Are you embarrassed to ask?

_____

_____

_____

_____

_____

_____

_____

_____

_____

_____

_____

_____

_____

5. How and where do you like to be touched? Do you even know?

_____

_____

_____

_____

_____

_____

_____

_____

_____

_____

_____

_____

6. Do you feel comfortable asking your partner these questions?

_____

_____

_____

_____

_____

_____

_____

_____

_____

_____

_____

_____

_____

_____

7. Do you or your partner have a special way to ask for sex?

_____

_____

_____

_____

_____

_____

_____

_____

_____

_____

_____

_____

_____

8. What happens when one person is too tired or disengaged?

_____

_____

_____

_____

_____

_____

_____

_____

_____

_____

_____

_____

_____

_____

9. How do you deal with this reaction?

10. Have you noticed if you and your partner have a favorite position? Have you discussed this with each other?

_____

_____

_____

_____

_____

_____

_____

_____

_____

_____

_____

_____

_____

_____

11. What is your favorite time to make love? Are you open to spontaneity?

_____

_____

_____

_____

_____

_____

_____

_____

_____

_____

_____

_____

_____

_____

12. How often would you like to have sex? When? Where?

_____

_____

_____

_____

_____

_____

_____

_____

_____

_____

_____

_____

_____

13. Do you ensure you are both satisfied?

14. Is there anything sexually you would like to try? What can we do to make our sex life better? Can you tell me? Can I tell you?

---

15. Is there a focus during sex on imperfect body image? Are we able to focus on what we do like about ourselves and each other?

_____

_____

_____

_____

_____

_____

_____

_____

_____

_____

_____

_____

16. Do you avoid touching yourself in a personal way? Why?

_____

_____

_____

_____

_____

_____

_____

_____

_____

_____

_____

_____

17. How can we make our bedroom into a place to play?

_____

_____

_____

_____

_____

_____

_____

_____

_____

_____

_____

_____

NOTES

I''ve been asked so many times; "Why am I not having an orgasm?"

Gd knows what he's talking about... Dim the lights. Forget about your imperfections. See yourself as the woman or man you want to be.

MAKING YOUR MOVE

WHAT ARE PHEROMONES? *Men's Tips*

Pheromones are chemical hormones produced by your skin. These chemicals carry with them a faint scent that informs humans of the best genetic match when choosing a mate.

So what does this have to do with attraction and sexuality? Well, Gentleman, it means that a woman reacts both physically and emotionally to your *scent*.

Prepare yourself for time alone with your woman. Shower up, practice good oral hygiene, find a scent that you know turns her on and no matter how tired you are, do not get into bed smelling like sweaty gym socks...

Need more info? Try out our Mens Short Course for healthy sexuality. www.thesecretsofjewishwomen.com

AROUSAL

Passion begins in the mind. When a woman feels passion, her body comes alive.

A woman needs to feel connected to feel desire. She needs to feel completely emotionally safe with you before she can feel safe sexually.

Many men are uneducated about the female body.

Study her body. Take note of what makes her feel good, where and when she likes to be touched.

Before initiating lovemaking with a woman who's been chasing children all day, give her a moment to relax and unwind. Show some understanding. Tend to the emotional aspects of love before the physical.

Familiarize yourself with specific pleasurable spots that you see she enjoys. Do you understand the female anatomy and know where her clitoris is located? Are you aware of how she likes to be aroused?

221

THE KISS

Everyone always remembers their first kiss. Clumsy, passionate, tender or juicy, the kiss matters. Lips have a great number of nerve endings. Those nerve endings can signal the brain to release a flood of feel good hormones.
You want that flood of hormones, trust me.
Be confident, read the signs and make the move. It doesn't matter if you've been married for ages.
Brush your teeth. Have a mint (especially if you smoke) because...
The kiss matters.
Touch her face, run your fingers through her hair and build anticipation. Hover over her lips and let the desire to touch build. Touch slowly, be in the moment. If you notice she moves her head back, or pulls away, you could be misreading signals. Any subtle movement backward is a signal to wait, slow down.
Proceed slowly, perhaps more time and talking is needed.
Continue to build a safe environment and then slowly try again.
This is absolutely not the time to go in for a feel.

Did you know that a man's saliva contains testosterone and that testosterone increases sex drive in a woman? The kiss really matters.
Practice makes perfect.

FEMALE ANATOMY

EXTERIOR

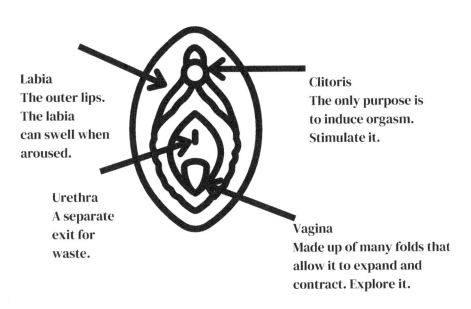

Labia
The outer lips.
The labia
can swell when
aroused.

Clitoris
The only purpose is
to induce orgasm.
Stimulate it.

Urethra
A separate
exit for
waste.

Vagina
Made up of many folds that
allow it to expand and
contract. Explore it.

Fallopian Tubes
Eggs are released from the ovaries and travel
through these tubes. Most times fertilization
and conception takes place here.

INTERIOR

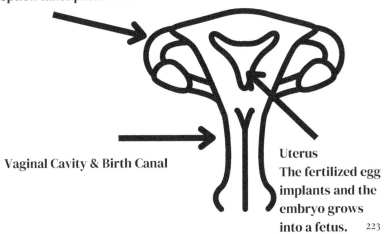

Vaginal Cavity & Birth Canal

Uterus
The fertilized egg
implants and the
embryo grows
into a fetus. 223

FOR MEN ON THEIR WEDDING NIGHT

Let's focus on the long awaited night. The memory of this first night will last forever.

The responsibility of our first time together, be it positive or negative, lies heavily on you, the man. It is critical to understand how vulnerable it is for a woman to be naked before her new husband. Suffice to say, if there is anything that you perceive that catches you off guard visually, keep it to yourself. Offer her wine, be attentive to her, and ask her if there's anything she needs or wants. Be charming and cute, make her smile. Let her disrobe herself when she is ready and go at her pace. You must control your urge to touch her in vulnerable areas. Practicing cognitively* speaking to yourself weeks before the wedding and making a conscious decision to maintain presence will help you with your urges and ease chaotic thoughts. Remember, she is going through a lot and so are you.

So, let's begin.

Remain dressed to a certain extent, keeping undergarments on. (t-shirt and briefs) This will ensure protection against getting overly excited and will enable you to remain focussed on your woman. The idea here is to be intent on pleasing her.

A suggestion for you would be to use coconut oil and to give your wife a massage. Start by touching the exposed areas including her head, neck, shoulders and arms. The goal is to relax her nervous system and build a sense of trust and safety. Sex without trust and safety leaves a woman feeling empty, lost and scared. This is extremely important to understand.

Check in with her to see if she's feeling relaxed. When the time is right you can also massage her back and legs. Do not remove her bra. Ask her if she's comfortable and how she's feeling. Inquiring after her wellbeing will let her know that you're present. Being responsive and interactive will diffuse the tension between you. When she removes her bra, breasts can be massaged firmly, (not too hard) slowly. No tickling, pulling or pinching. This is not the time for you to put your mouth on them.

Get into the mindset that this night is for exploration and building trust. We want to leave this experience looking forward to being together again.

Lay down on the bed close to her, side by side. Lean in to begin kissing her. (We have a whole section on the kiss. Your breath must be fresh and your teeth clean).

As the passion increases... (still in your briefs) You can then take your hand and put it between her legs, gently exploring the outer area and indicating her to open and to remove her underwear. We assume that your nails are trimmed, cut and clean.

After massaging the outer area, reach for the coconut oil to lubricate the area inside. Slip a finger towards the top and start investigating where her clitoris is. Sandwiched between two layers of skin you will feel a hard pea shaped object. You don't want to overly massage the clitoris itself. Apply firm but gentle pressure in a circular motion around it, not directly, so as not to cause irritation. No direct rubbing.

Expecting her to have an orgasm under these circumstances is unrealistic. Do not take this personally. You will have many years B"H to get this right. Tonight, taking this very needed time to learn for yourself the wonders of your wifes body and that you are capable of being in control will pay off big time. This is how to develop true self-confidence.

At this point, ask her for consent and then remove your briefs. The position is face to face. Your hands will be on either side of her head above her shoulders. Get into a woman's push-up position with your knees on the bed in between her legs and your toes curled to propel yourself forward. She should then take your penis in her hand and guide you inside a little at a time. At this point you can drop down on your forearms and get closer to her.

This will accomplish two things. Firstly, this position will keep you securely stable on top of her with no need to fumble around trying to put yourself inside. It also gives her the security to let you in at a pace that she can control and is comfortable with. Once you have entered she will put her legs around your thighs and rest her heels on the back of your calves. Practicing this position will enable her to have an orgasm by pulling you into her vertically creating friction on her clitoris. This will also ensure that you do not fall out and lose seed.

After the fact... There are different opinions about this moment, please ask your Rav.

We suggest; hold her, do not get up. Stay there until she moves first. Ask her if you're too heavy on her. When you do move, lay side by side holding her.

At this point you will need to separate.

Ask, "Is there anything I can do for you?"

If she starts to cry or has an emotional reaction, stay still. You are now in a state of Niddah. This is a very hard moment for both of you. Your first reaction might be to shut down emotionally, don't. If you can, keep it light and maintain connection.

Be proud of yourself. You took your time and showed true self-control. She will appreciate and remember this forever.

Talk about how you're feeling and ask about her. Expressing yourself is what intimacy is all about.
Don't take her silence personally, she wants to be with you as much as you want to be with her.

The foundation of marriage is more than just physical touch. You can touch another person with your intention.

*Cognitive Behavioral Therapy
Thinking about changing a thought will do nothing to change a behavior unless an action is attached to it. Repeating a statement out loud is an action. Writing is an action. Here are some positive statements you can make, write them down and say them out loud.

"I am in control of my urges"
"My wife's needs come first"
"I wish to please my wife before myself"
"I want my wife to feel comfortable and safe"

Your prefrontal cortex, the decision making part of the brain, will take the statement with the action attached and create a new behavior. It must be done before going into the actual situation. Repeating the action and the statement will install the new thought.

THE KISS

Let's talk about what to do:

- Build tension for the kiss.
- Lean in and pause.
- Look into his eyes.
- Feel the breath and hold close without touching.
- Slightly open your mouth.
- Start the kiss slowly, softening your lips, slightly open, without tension.
- Don't go in with your tongue just yet.

Change the pace. This signals variety and increases the urge. When he feels you getting turned on- he gets turned on. Increase the intensity, and pressure with your lips. Tilt your head slowly to either side.

Change the pace again, pulling back slightly. Pausing between kissing and grazing lips will stimulate excitement.
Think to yourself, how do you want to be kissed?
Should I Initiate the kiss?
Can you lean in for the kiss and get close enough so this can happen?
Can you guide him where you want him to kiss you?

Now, let's talk about the clitoris...

During penetrative vaginal sex there is generally not enough stimulation to orgasm.
There is research that suggests most women cannot orgasm at all during penetration. This is a myth. If you would like to be able to orgasm in this position, here is some advice.
In order to understand why this is so, we have to understand where the clitoris is located.
First and foremost, getting to know your own body is a must. We suggest you take a mirror and look down there. The tip of the clitoris is north and feels like a hardened shape the size of a pea. Its head is sandwiched between folds of skin above and beneath it. The urethra is below, where urine is excreted and further south is the vaginal opening.
For best results, we suggest manually stimulating the area with your hand and some coconut oil in the shower prior to being with your husband. This stimulation accelerates your physical desire.
After some time of foreplay, and hopefully achieving orgasm through your partner manually stimulating you, you may begin to have intercourse (face to face). Your partner will get into a woman's push-up position between your legs and he will be facing you. His knees are bent on the bed and hands on either side of your shoulders for stabilization.

Your legs go around his thighs, the soles of your feet resting on his calves. Bring him into you by way of the back of his knees.

While resting the soles of your feet on his calves, pull him towards you, you are creating the vertical friction required for a penetrative orgasm.

While your legs are wrapped around him, heels resting on his calves, you're also using his body and hips to squeeze your thighs against him and ever so slightly elevating your pelvis. We do not suggest using a pillow for this position. With your pelvis slightly elevated, body leveraged around him, your heels on the back of his calves; you can do pelvic floor contractions to enhance the sensation for both of you.

Tips for the night of the wedding and something to keep in mind: He will lose his stabilized position with his hands by trying to put himself inside you. To avoid this, use your hand to guide him in by taking hold of his penis. You have an opportunity to manually stimulate him if he's yet to be fully erect. This will also allow you to control the pace of his entry and minimize pain and discomfort.

Remember, don't forget the coconut oil.

A note to the Kallah: You may experience some irritation after your first encounter. This is no reason to avoid intercourse when it's appropriate. Your husband could lay behind you and enter your vagina from the back i.e. "spooning". This could be more comfortable and lead to unexpected pleasure and stimulation of the G-Spot.

Health note: After intercourse, it is advisable to urinate, this will return the vagina back to a healthy pH balance and help prevent urinary tract and yeast infections.

What's all this talk about date night?...

Try asking open ended questions. Get him talking so that you can respond.
The attraction process begins non-verbally. A simple smile, the look of longing in your eyes is a great way to spark interest. Gaze at his lips when he's speaking to you. Flirt with him by finding something on his clothing to touch. Don't be afraid to feel awkward with the silence.
When he initiates contact with you, pull back ever so slightly, this will slow him down while maintaining non verbal cues that you are open to him.

Say things like: "I'm having such a good time". Move closer to him and put one hand on his chest, slide the other hand to the back of his neck and run your fingers through his hair.
Pay close attention to how he is responding, without second guessing yourself. Press yourself against him and gently get close enough for a kiss.

Above all, be present, in the moment and have fun.

FLIRTING

Don't assume that men know that you're attracted to them or that they know what's going on in your body and in your mind. Men are not mind readers. Trust me when I say if you give them a window into how you're thinking and how you're feeling, it is going to make a huge difference for them. The more you give them an understanding of your desires, the more that's going to turn him on.

The second principle I want to share with you is the power of future pacing.
This is really fun, you use specific phrases and methods, to draw him into the experience you're looking forward to sharing with him later, whatever that may be.

Know that if you master future pacing and you use it effectively, his brain will release dopamine and it's going to get him primed for what's to come. The beautiful thing about future pacing is that you can use it over an unlimited distance.

The first way to do this is by giving him a future feeling statement of something that you're looking forward to experiencing with him later. A great example of this would be, *I can't wait to be with you tonight.* This will absolutely light up his entire body, he will start visualizing and thinking about how wonderful it's going to feel to do that.

Remember going back to the first principle we talked about is that men love knowing how their actions turn you on. Men love being acknowledged for what they're doing. One of the greatest ways that you can acknowledge a man for his actions is by letting him know how much he excites you.

The second way to use this principle is in a future action statement. And that's where you share something that you're looking forward to doing to him or that you're looking forward to him doing to you.

Third, is a present sensation statement. You're giving him the understanding of what you are presently experiencing right now. This can be arousing for a man and is going to elicit a similar sort of reaction from him. He's probably going to share what he's feeling too, which brings us to the fourth way to use this framework...

A present sensation question. This is where you ask him in a warm, inviting, sensual way what he's feeling and experiencing in the middle of this conversation. Then you hold space for his response and play off of it.

So you could say something like,

So how does it make you feel to know that we will be together tonight?

And part of what's so cool about this is that you're actually getting him to connect with his body and open up to you vulnerably about what it is that he's feeling and experiencing. It may be at the physical level, but it is a type of vulnerability that a lot of times men don't have experience discussing. So this really is you showing up as the initiator of the relationship, getting him to speak to you in a more intimate manner and building and deepening the connection between the two of you. 233

Another great way to get a man to drop into his sexuality or sensuality and take the conversation to the next level is through asking sexy questions.

A fun type of question within hypotheticals is the, would you rather question.

Would you rather have sex in bed or out of bed if you had to pick one?

There are a million would you rather questions that are out there. They're a really fun way to get a man to open up and start thinking and talking about sex in a playful way.

The idea is to build a connection with him and get his motor running. Just remember that the key to asking a man questions about sex is to always show up soft, warm, inviting and curious. He needs to know that when you're asking him these questions, that this is a safe space, that you are not doing an inquisition. You want to make sure that you have created a level of trust with him or else he might not give you a full and open response.

All of this can be done through voice memo or voice text. It will have a completely different level of response from your man. So, leverage the power of your voice and don't be afraid to send him any of these texts.

This allows him to feel the energy and the sensuality behind your words and create a much more intimate connection with you. Just know that exchanging flirty or sexy voice memos is a really powerful way to build sexual connection, create deeper intimacy, build tension, and take your back and forth dialogue to a completely different level and make him very turned on.

234

The goal is to build tension and anticipation with him. You want to do that with pacing. We want to build anticipation throughout the day.

So ladies, if you can remember these three principles, you're going to be able to effortlessly turn on your man no matter how far apart you may be.

THE ART OF TOUCH

Touch is the gateway to seduction. How and where you touch your man can send signals of love and desire straight to his core. Here I will walk you through each zone of the body and give some suggestions for seduction.

Upper Zone... Head, Neck, Shoulders, Chest

Touch his hair lightly, engaging the nerve endings in his scalp. Move to his ears with a very light massage. Do not stick your tongue in his ear. Run your fingernails through the back of his hair and whisper in his ear. Tell him he looks hot and how attractive he is. Men also need compliments. Stroke his lips lightly with your fingertips.

The neck holds a lot of daily tension. Touch lightly and massage to release. Make eye contact with him, he may kiss you. Lightly tickle the back of his neck but if he laughs- stop

Kiss his neck below each ear, not too wet of a kiss, light and passionately.

Engaging the shoulders with a massage is also a great way to release physical tension, build sexual anticipation, relax him and get him talking. Ask an open ended question so that you can react to the story with light touching and words of affirmation.

Men hold a lot of their power in their chest. When you see your man with his shoulders back and chest out, he's ready to take on anything. Laying your head on his chest makes him feel like your protector. Lightly but firmly touch his chest and stomach, you don't want to tickle him. This will slow the nervous system and bring him into the moment.

Middle Zone... Stomach, lower back, hands and wrists

The wrists and hands are little known pleasure zones. Sit side by side and lightly touch his inner wrist, proceed to massage his hand.
His stomach and lower back are connected to his pelvis. Massaging his lower back and spine will awaken this zone.You can lightly place your hand on his lower back when walking to signal your attraction.
There are tons of nerve endings around the belly button, circle it with varying degrees of pressure (not too hard or lightly).
Kissing around the belly button can also be a big turn on when the moment is close at hand.

Lower Zone...Legs, feet
Have him lay on his stomach. Start at the bottom of his feet with a gentle massage. Feel free to use the recommended coconut oil. Move up the legs, behind the knees to his inner thighs. Massage up and down the thigh with varying pressure.

THE FEMALE ORGASM

Why should we have orgasms? Why is it so important?

Orgasms give life, make you feel alive.

Orgasms slow down aging and keep you young. Why do you think that is?

One of the biggest differences between animals and humans is our ability to enjoy sex.

Animals only mate to procreate. Our brain thinks every time we have sex we are procreating. Internally the brain signals hormones to be released for fertility.

If you're 50/60 years old and still orgasming you're clearly not having any babies right? The brain doesn't know the difference and still thinks it has to keep you young.

Every time you orgasm, the brain signals your body to make killer cells that fight cancer, depression and illness. The more you have sex

(good sex) the more your body creates these cells and hormones.

Even if it's self induced, you're sending a subliminal signal to your brain that's readying your body to make a baby, and nature responds by keeping you young enough to care for that supposed baby.

If pushing off aging isn't reason enough...

Try it for pain management! Have a headache? Have an orgasm!! Your body will send the blood from your headache down below and voila! No more headache.

Frequent orgasms release a powerful bonding hormone called oxytocin, that keeps you and your partner close.

So, why aren't we having all these amazing orgasms and great sex?

I listen to couples all the time who are very much in love but not having a lot of sex.

We're having less sex than our grandmothers did, why is that?

We are so busy these days, there's so much going on, so many distractions that sex becomes another item on the to-do list.

The media has also done a terrible disservice to women. Every year there is another body part to hate.

Thighs that touch? Men love that

A woman's sweat? Men find that sexy

The world is telling you to look like a younger and younger girl. With hair removal, no curves, designer vaginas. We are so preoccupied with perfection it's almost impossible to relax into ourselves.

I'll tell you a secret... When a man is turned on, your body is perfect to him.

Your man wants someone who is warm and receptive. Let go of the obsession with the body you're presenting.

TURN OFF THE LIGHTS!

We're not having enough sex because we're not feeling desirable enough.

Let me tell you why.

Desire begins in the mind. This is where we need to do our work.

239

Sexual attraction begins here, so does the power to orgasm. The sexiest organ you have is your brain. This is where all of the feel good chemicals begin to take shape. It is the place where every fertile element of your life actually lives.

Here's a news flash... Your orgasm is your responsibility. Not your partners.

Our husbands are not psychic. Unless you find the words to say what pleases you, it will be nearly impossible for him to do so.

You need to learn what feels good and be able to express it.

What you like and don't like needs to be communicated at the proper time, gently. Preferably in a moment of closeness outside the bedroom. Have patience and go slow.

Intimacy and desire are not the same thing.
An exciting sex life involves having pleasure, excitement, drama, mystery and even a little naughtiness.
Having an intimate relationship is friendship, safety, and predictability.
Predictability is the killer of desire. The same thing over and over and over will create boredom.
Mix it up! Try different things, keep it exciting! Get creative and curious.

The bridge between intimacy and desire is fantasy.
(see fantasy chapter)

Pregnancy, exhaustion, work and children will take up most of your mental energy. Believing that you're no longer attracted to each other is a result of your thinking patterns . If you believe you're not attracted, it will become reality. You will start looking for proof that supports these beliefs. Beware of these thought patterns and work diligently and consciously to change them. Remember when you first met? The fantasies you had then held all the potential and are what you have to work towards to remember. Take some time each day to do this, those memories are there you just need to retrieve them.

The same is true for all negative thought patterns around sex. If the mind says "no", the body follows.

<u>Thoughts come before all else</u>.

A belief starts with a simple thought. A thought that we think all the time becomes a belief.

Thought creates your feelings, which generates your actions. Repeated actions become a behavior. So, thinking "I'm not attractive, I can't orgasm, there is something wrong with me" will soon become the reality in which you live.

When you start becoming aware of your thinking and think purposefully "I am attractive, I can orgasm, there is nothing wrong with me." Join these thoughts together with an action and your body will respond.

The mind doesn't have any preference in what you're telling it. Good or bad, true or false. It lets those thoughts be and every thought you have has an emotional effect on your body. You want to make good friends with yourself.

When you tell yourself that you are sexy, and you do something nice for yourself, you are switching on an incredible life force.
So, switch it up, speak life and love into yourself.

PELVIC FLOOR EXERCISES TO ENHANCE ORGASM

A little background... Pelvic floor exercises (Kegels) are an essential part of women's health. They help to strengthen the muscles that support the bladder, uterus and recturm. Doing pelvic floor exercises will prevent conditions such as incontinence, prolapse and help to achieve stronger orgasm.

One effective way to do pelvic floor exercises is by squeezing a ball between the knees. To begin, find a small ball or pillow that you can comfortably squeeze. Lie down on your back with knees bent and feet flat on the floor. Place the ball between your knees and gently squeeze it as you exhale. Hold the squeeze for a few seconds then release as you inhale. You will feel the hollow of your stomach press down on the floor. Repeat this exercise for 10-15 repetitions, taking care not to over exert yourself. As you become more comfortable you can gradually increase the length of time you hold the squeeze. Squeezing a ball between your knees is an effective way to engage the pelvic floor muscles, vaginal wall, while also working the inner thigh muscles. It is a low impact exercise that can be done at home, making it an ideal option for women who may not have time to attend a gym or fitness class. In addition to pelvic floor exercises there are other ways to support pelvic health including maintaining a healthy weight and avoiding constipation.
Utilizing this exercise while having penetrative sex will enhance orgasm for both of you.

Sarah Fraser

CHAPTER 12

THE
Mik ah

Many women relate to going to the Mikvah as a chore. They feel that it is an imposition on them in order to have intimacy with their husbands, and this often brings with it no small amount of resentment. Ironically, this perspective, though not uncommon, stems from a total misconception about what the Mikvah is actually about and who it is for.

Most of the time in our waking state of reality we tend to overlook the fact that in the physical world there are parallel worlds going on simultaneously. There are natural forces influencing one another in both realities.
Mikvah is one of these parallel realities.

Rabbi Aryeh Kaplan illuminates the points in the following quotations from the English translation of "Waters Of Eden"

*References to male gender are also meant to include women.

How does man purify himself and remove himself from a state of spiritual uncleanliness? How does he reassociate himself with Eden? The purification is primarily through water, through immersion in the Mikvah. Water is the primary connection we have with the Garden of Eden. All the water in the world has its roots in the River that emerged from Eden. Even though the person cannot re-enter the Garden of Eden itself, whenever he associates himself with these rivers- or any other water- he is re-establishing his link with Eden. This also explains why the Mikvah must be linked to natural water. Water must come to the Mikvah from its natural state, and must not come into contact with man in his state of spiritual exile. Similarly, it must not pass through anything that is capable of being defiled, since this would also break the direct link with the River of Eden. The Torah tells us that Gd planted a Garden, and in it, the Tree Of Knowledge of Good and Evil. With it, the possibility was created that man would sin, and be evicted from Eden. Thus, even before Gd placed man in Eden, He established a link between the Garden and the world outside, namely the River which emerged from Eden. Rather, it is an important statement regarding man's condition in the world outside of Eden. Even though man has been expelled from Eden, a link remains. The concept of Mikvah is very closely associated with this link. Mikvah alludes to the "waters of knowledge" that will ultimately encompass all mankind. To the primitive mind, which had no idea of the inner workings of a womb, the very idea that a woman should lose a portion of her vital fluids was both bizarre and frightening. They could not explain it logically and attributed it to some evil force.We see that all our biological logic and sophistication does not really help us understand this natural phenomena.

Another large area where human imperfection is evident is in the area of sex and reproduction. Rather than being a simple, natural, biological function, sex is the source of man's greatest compulsions and frustrations. Man's innate nature demands that he should have psychological conflicts with regard to sex. One obvious area where man's lack of sexual integration is apparent is with respect to his attitude towards his body. One of the reasons sex is so holy is because it has the ability to accomplish something that is beyond the power of any other human function- namely, drawing a soul down to the world, and producing a living human being. Incidentally, this explains why Gds covenant with Avraham involved circumcision- an indelible mark on the organ of reproduction . As the father of the "chosen people " Avraham and his children would now be able use this organ to bring the holiest souls into the world. The covenant of circumcision was one of the things that elevated Avraham from the fallen state resulting from the expulsion from Eden. On a simpler level, Niddah is a sign of the imperfection of the human reproductive process. Therefore, the purification and rectification of Niddah must return to the perfected "womb" that is the Mikvah.

The husband-wife bond is essential for the rearing of human children. On the other hand, the very basic and essential relationship between husband and wife can fall apart through something as undramatic as simple boredom. The monthly separation tends to renew the sexual relationship and thus stabilize the marriage bond. On another level, the fact that husband and wife cannot have any physical contact during the days of separation forces them to look upon each other as human beings, rather than as mere sex objects. ²⁴⁷

- The Mikvah must consist of water, no other liquids can be used.
- The Mikvah must either be built into the ground, or be an integral part of a building attached to the ground. It cannot consist of any vessel that can be disconnected and carried away, such as a tub, vat or barrel.
- The water of a Mikvah cannot be running or flowing. The only exception is a natural spring, or river whose water is derived mainly from springs.
- The water of the Mikvah cannot be drawn. That is, it cannot be brought to the Mikvah through direct human intervention.
- The water cannot be channeled to the Mikvah through anything that can become unclean.
- The Mikvah must contain at least 40 Sa 'ah, approximately 200 gallons.

All this indicates that the entire body must come in contact with the water. There is a general rule that if something is mixed with twice its volume it is considered to be nullified. The largest human body is 20 Sa'ah. Therefore, the amount of water necessary to nullify this body is double this, or is 40 Sa 'ah.

Water, being the prototype fluid, is therefore the one substance that primarily represents change and instability. Life is a unique combination of change and permanence. A living thing is constantly changing, and yet at the same time retains its identity. Before creation change did not exist. Gd dwells in a realm above time, and the concept of change does not apply to Him in any way whatsoever. Therefore, one of the first ingredients of creation had to be the very concept of change.

The Torah describes the world at the beginning of creation by saying (Genesis 1:2) "The earth was formless and chaotic, with darkness on the face of the deep, and Gd's spirit causing motion on the face of the water."

Most important, we see that water itself represents the change and flow toward Gd's goal. When a person immerses himself in a Mikvah, he immerses himself spiritually in the basic concept of change itself. Man's ego represents the element of his permanence, and therefore, when he is totally immersed in the concept of change, his ego is nullified. Thus, when he emerges from the Mikvah, he is in a total state of renewal and rebirth.

The past is history and cannot be changed. We have no way of even touching the future. Therefore, the arena of action, where all change takes place, is the present.

"Gd (HaShem) is Israel's Mikvah" Just as the Mikvah purifies the unclean, so Gd purifies Israel. -Mishneh, Yoma 8:9

In this verse, the word Mikvah actually means "hope". But what is hope? It actually represents our feelings toward an event in the future. When we hope that some future event will happen, we are dealing with something that is beyond the barrier of time. We therefore say that our hope is Hashem-The name. We use this name when we are speaking of Gd. As we know, the word Mikvah actually means a "gathering". Taken in this context, it is also a gathering of time- a gathering of past and future into the present, making them both accessible to us. The ability to transcend the bonds of time, on the other hand, is the ultimate freedom.

249

Therefore, when a person enters the Mikvah, he enters a state where past, present and future are all "gathered together" and is therefore ultimately free. He is no longer bound by past or future, but exists in an absolute present, which is the one instant of time over which man has absolute control. Therefore, the freedom of Mikvah overcomes the lack of freedom associated with Tumah.

Scripture speaks of this when it says, "Who can bring the clean out of the unclean, if not the One"

On a personal note:

Gd seems inaccessible to us, at this time.
We have no temple or prophecy. The mikvah has been and remains, an unbroken, continuous and total connection to Gd.
Gd is everything. He is the air we breathe and the water you drink. 80% of the water in your body is Gd.
Gd is the water you are immersing in.
The specifications and detail of the mikvah have been set in such a way by Gd, to facilitate this state for us to access him; and has been, for thousands of years.
At this time, in order to access Gd in this physical world, we do so through intimacy with one another, and through using the mikvah. You are in a womb for that moment you are under the water.
We have an opportunity, as Jewish women, to undergo transformation and be close to Gd in a realm where there is no past, present or future, which is where he resides. When you submerge yourself, and pray for yourself and all those you care about; these prayers are going directly to Gd.
Yes, we need to use the mikvah to be with our husbands intimately, but we are NOT doing this *solely for* our husbands.
We are doing this for ourselves.
Disrobing in front of the mikvah attendant can be unsettling. Why waste these precious moments thinking about the mikvah attendant, when you have such an important opportunity for spiritual connection?

CONCLUSION

Most issues that arise in a marriage are a reflection of what is happening (or not happening) in the bedroom. Completing this learning path is not a guarantee that your relationship will be free of challenges. True growth is always tested. Life will test you and your relationship. The extent of your commitment to one another will help you rise to any occasion. At the core of commitment is remaining together and enduring adversity. Learning to respond differently in the face of conflict will free you from your past. Now that you have read and answered all the questions, done all the work, and think you know your partner... go back and use this workbook again, and again, and then again. When intimacy issues present, ask yourself which of these topics in the learning path need to be revisited. There is no shame in reaching out to seek professional help. This shows respect for the importance of the relationship.

the secrets of jewish women

ACKNOWLEDGMENTS:

I would like to thank my Husband for being so supportive; and my team, Candace Ker for her invaluable contributions and art direction along with Ruth Jankowitz for her insights and patience. I could not have done this without you guys.

A NOTE FROM SARAH

This course of 12 weeks was created to teach couples fundamental ways to relate in a healthy relationship and regain the motivation and reason they came together in the first place.

It is imperative for the Kallah teacher and Chosson teachers to have connection throughout training, so that they teach the same things.

Ideally this course needs to be given within the first few months of marriage.

This course is an essential part of wedding preparations and needs to be prioritized along with the band, the hall, the wig, dress, guests etc.

We all need to do our part in strengthening Jewish families.

For additional resources and referrals please visit
www.thesecretsofjewishwomen.com

Sarah Fraser

Made in the USA
Middletown, DE
24 February 2024

49839435R00146